Radio in the Digital Age

Digital Media and Society Series

Radio in the Digital Age

ANDREW DUBBER

polity

First edition published in 2013 by Polity Press

Polity Press
65 Bridge Street
Cambridge CB2 1UR, UK

Polity Press
350 Main Street
Malden, MA 02148, USA

ISBN-13: 978-0-7456-6196-4
ISBN-13: 978-0-7456-6197-1(pb)

A catalogue record for this book is available from the British Library.

Typeset in 10.25 on 13 pt FF Scala by
Servis Filmsetting Ltd, Stockport, Cheshire
Printed and bound by Clays Ltd, St Ives

For further information on Polity, visit our website: www.politybooks.com

Contents

Acknowledgements

In a way, I've been writing this book for over 20 years. It's only the typing of it that has happened in the last 12 months. Over those two decades, many people have shaped my thoughts about radio, about the meanings of shifts in technological environments and about how to codify and explain my ideas about them. To single those people out here and explain why each was so important to me would cause the Acknowledgements to exceed the length of the book. Some of those people provided mentorship (whether they knew it or not), others ideas, practical assistance and expert advice. Others have written the words that I quote and refer to in this work, without which I would not be able to think what I think. More have provided the incredibly professional services that have turned my rough manuscript into the polished and finished work you hold in your hands. Still more provided me with the support, indulgence and space I needed to finish this book to a deadline that happened to coincide with some rather significant events in my life.

I'm incredibly grateful to them all, especially to those I'm proud to call my friends and my family, who didn't just make this book possible, but also gave me the best reasons to write it – and even better ones to finish it.

Naturally, I want to thank everyone – but I'll make sure to do so in person. Repeatedly.

However, there is one person I can't thank in person, and so wish to do so publicly.

This book is dedicated to the late John Haynes, who not only introduced me to the phenomenon of the 'thinking radio practitioner', but also provided me with the best example I have ever encountered. John took me under his wing at the beginning of my career and showed me that radio, technology, culture and the human mind were all things worthy of close and thoughtful examination. He planted all of the seeds. This book is just one season's crop.

Abbreviations

AAC	advanced audio coding
A&R	artists and repertoire
ADAT	Alesis Digital Audio Tape
AM	amplitude modulation
API	application programming interface
CB radio	Citizen Band radio
CEG	Consumer Expert Group
CHR	Contemporary Hit Radio
DAB	digital audio broadcasting
DAT	digital audio tape
DAW	digital audio workstation
EBU	European Broadcasting Union
FCC	Federal Communications Commission
FM	frequency modulation
FTP	File Transfer Protocol
IBOC	in-band, on-channel
IP	Internet Protocol
IRC	Internet Relay Chat
ISDN	Integrated Services Digital Network
kHz	kilohertz
LDBK	Laid Back Radio
LPFM	low-power FM
MB	megabyte
MED	Ministry for Economic Development (now Ministry of Business)
NAB	National Association of Broadcasters
NRK	Norsk rikskringkasting
OfCom	Office of Communications

PCM	pulse code modulator
PRS	Performing Rights Society
PRX	Public Radio Exchange
R&D	research and development
RAJAR	Radio Joint Audience Research
RBDS	Radio Broadcast Data System
RCA	Radio Corporation of America
RCS	Radio Computing Services
RDS	radio data system
RIAA	Recording Industry Association of America
RSS	Rich Site Summary
SD	Secure Digital
SMS	Short Message Service
TB	terabyte
UGC	user-generated content
USB	Universal Serial Bus
VHS	Video Home System
VoIP	Voice over Internet Protocol
XML	Extensible Markup Language

CHAPTER ONE

What is Radio?

So much has changed in radio since I started. You know, the whole technological revolution that's gone on. I remember doing a show with Steve Lamacq in the early days and the title was 'What is the Internet?' and there will be archive of us somewhere going 'Just explain how this works then? What? Really?' and we must sound incredibly stupid and naïve, but then everybody was – we all were. When I started broadcasting, you got letters from people. That was the way they communicated. And you spoke to your audience. Now there are just so many different ways of people communicating with you. It's constant. It's this barrage. And it's a two-way street. They're texting you, you're texting them, you're tweeting them, they're tweeting you, it's Facebook, it's everything. There are cameras in the radio studios. When I went into radio I was fairly shy. I used to embrace the time you could go in and you could just wear a tracksuit and no makeup and that was great. But now you're thinking, 'Oh no, actually, there's a camera there and you have to put a bit of makeup on.' So it's just such a different medium. But at the same time . . . it's you and it's a microphone and it's somebody listening, wherever they are around the world. So radio, I think, still essentially remains the same.

Jo Whiley
(interviewed on Paul Gambaccini's 'Music in the Air: History of Music Radio', BBC Radio 2, episode 6 of 6, first broadcast 18 December 2012)

Introduction

Before I became a radio academic I was a radio practitioner; and so, like many people who study and write about radio, I draw upon both sets of professional experiences. The benefit of this is that it ensures our analyses are influenced and informed by both our experience of the 'real world' of radio and our arms-length academic research. However, it also presents the danger that we will start our study with some (so-called) truisms about radio that have not been tested through intellectual rigour or painstaking analysis, but that have instead been arrived at through the discourse of pragmatic and routine practices. In other words, there are many things about radio that have come through the academic tradition and reside within the canon of radio studies literature, but that have their origin in things that are simply 'known' or 'obvious' to radio practitioners.

It is important, then, that I recognise that my own understanding of radio, like that of many radio academics, originates very much in the world of practice; in the discourse of radio professionals; in the day-to-day experience of making, presenting and producing radio programmes, programming music formats, writing and recording commercial copy. I am, perhaps, an entirely typical radio academic in this respect: I try to draw upon my previous professional background as well as my ongoing involvement in radio today.

It is perhaps also important to start with some reflection on how we come to study radio, because this ensures that we do not forget that the understanding we have of radio, of media, of technology and of society is a personal and cultural understanding, and not simply an accumulation of objective facts. It is filtered through a veil of life experiences, moments of personal profoundness, and the unique set of baggage and contextual frames we bring to bear on the object of analysis. In short, we can never quite become the dispassionate and aloof intellectuals who observe and interrogate a subject while bringing nothing to bear on that observation themselves. I am instead persuaded by the anthropological tradition of analysis, which attempts to give a voice to the objects of analysis themselves, to get out of the way as much as possible, but also to admit to the undeniable fact that the storyteller cannot but shape the narrative. It is with this in mind that I introduce myself in what, in another context, might seem an unnecessarily comprehensive and personal manner. With that in mind, I hope the reader will indulge the following personal history, in the hopes that it might add context and coherence to the content of this book.

Geographically speaking, I grew up and lived a significant proportion of my life in Auckland, New Zealand, but it seems to me that it was, in large part, radio that provided the environment within which that life took place. It wasn't time to walk to primary school until Merv Smith had chatted to MacHairy the Scottish spider just after the 8 o'clock news on 1ZB (1080 kHz on the AM band) and when I got there, if we were lucky, it was a day on which the 'Programmes for Schools' were broadcast, and we were given the opportunity to listen to stories as well as sing and clap, along with New Zealand children all over the country, led by the radio presenters and guided by our 'Programmes for Schools' workbooks.

Each year, my family would go on holiday to a beach house at Stanmore Bay in Whangaparoa, and I'd always be secretly pleased when it was too wet to go to the seaside because, over the Christmas and New Year summer break, the National Programme on Radio 1YA would play old episodes of BBC radio comedies like *The Navy Lark, Dad's Army, Round the Horne, I'm Sorry I'll Read That Again* and *The Goons*. I learned to play cribbage while laughing at Eccles and Bluebottle in a small, slopey-floored wooden house by the sea, as the rain came down outside. And at the end of our vacation, on the way home each year, we listened to Casey Kasem's syndicated American Top 40 year-end chart show on the car radio. I have a particularly strong memory of it having been a close-run thing, that one year, between Andy Gibb's 'Shadow Dancing' (which I loved) and Meco's disco version of the 'Star Wars Theme/Cantina Band' (which my 11-year-old tastes interpreted as innovative, engagingly derivative, but essentially problematic in terms of authenticity); and the revelation of the top spot on the US hit parade was a source of tremendous anticipation and excitement. Of course, now that I come to research and refresh these

memories, Google assures me that this never actually happened
– and that those two songs weren't even in the charts in the same
year. We should not perhaps be surprised by this, memory being
a construction and a narrative that we use to make sense of our
worlds. It's a 'truth' rather than something that is strictly factual.
However, the fact that we do this is significant in the context of
this book, and it's important to bear in mind right upfront that
perception and understanding are malleable, mutable and con-
tingent phenomena that may or may not be strictly related to the
ontological reality of things.

Throughout the rest of the year, every Sunday morning, I'd
listen as Don Linden played audio stories from a deep archive
of primarily American children's records that included *Molly
Whuppie, Gerald McBoingBoing, Sparky and the Talking Train,
Flick the Fire Engine, Little Toot, Gossamer Wump* and (the British
contribution) *Spike Milligan's Badjelly the Witch*, a musical story
written and performed by Milligan, which – like the song
'Snoopy's Christmas', which has dominated the airwaves in
December in New Zealand since the year I was born – is inex-
plicably little known in its UK home. It was engrossing, it fired
the imagination – and the way I remember it, it was pretty much
at the centre of my childhood. In fact, arguably, radio and music
have been what I've hung most of my memories off – real or
imagined. That makes it pretty powerful stuff, in my experience
– which, let's not forget, is what this is.

And then, after a while, I discovered another setting on
my grandparents' portable transistor radio receiver: shortwave.
There, among all the static, if you held the aerial just right, were
distant voices, strange music and people talking to each other
in foreign languages. It's a cliché, of course, to say that I was
'transported', but I don't really know another way to describe that
feeling, sitting on the front porch, hearing for the first time just
how big the rest of the world was.

In my early teens I was a fan of rock music stations Radio
Hauraki and 1251ZM (as it was known then) in equal measure. I
knew the names of all of the presenters, and I even wrote a letter

once to Hauraki, offering ideas for competitions. The music was, of course, central to all this. Radio was my main source of music listening. My parents had records at home, but I was quick to figure out that Roger Whittaker, Andy Williams and Helen Reddy didn't speak to me or for me, and so radio provided access to what, I imagined, represented me and connected me to a set of likeminded peers.

My radio listening grew to levels of active fandom, to the extent that I believed that I had figured out the playlist rotates to a high degree of accuracy; and I believed that I could reasonably confidently predict when, for instance, the B52s song 'Rock Lobster' would turn up again. Of course, I didn't know they were called 'rotates', or even that there was such a thing as a playlist – but I could tell that the presenters obviously liked some of the same records that I liked, and they seemed to play those records with predictable regularity. And even if my predictions were off (and they often were), I was content that, given that we shared such a bond of musical tastes – with only a few inexplicable deviations here and there – they were bound to play my favourite songs sooner rather than later.

The first album I ever chose for myself in a record shop was paid for by a voucher won in a phone-in competition. I selected David Bowie's *Scary Monsters (and Super Creeps)* album – but I must have spent a good half hour torn between that and Donna Summer's *The Wanderer*, while my father waited in the aisles of Jim's Record Spot in Panmure as I made what I knew to be a critical decision in my life of music fandom. Around that same time, there was a late (way past my bedtime) Sunday night programme on 1ZM, which, as I recall, was essentially about the apocalypse. It was part documentary, part speculative fiction, and partly an excuse to string a bunch of different songs together in an interesting way. The programme, the name of which is lost to memory, related all the ways in which we were likely to die imminently, collectively and absolutely as a species. Of course, I listened under the covers with a transistor radio and a terribly unreliable flashlight, as kids do. The programme featured all the popular nuclear paranoia of the time, as well as a lot of terrifying scenarios from religion and mythology. I remember vividly that the development of barcodes as a techno-cultural phenomenon was cited as evidence of something in the Book of Revelations; the Cold War was at its height, a planet-obliterating World War 3 was an historical inevitability and we were only 'Minutes to Midnight' on the Doomsday clock. Moreover – if you counted the number of letters in Ronald Wilson Reagan's name, you got 666. These chilling facts and coincidences were presented in such a way as to provide a compelling reason to play the song 'Games without Frontiers' by Peter Gabriel to an already emotionally heightened teen audience. That series provided not only my first hearing of that and some other songs I love to this day, but also the occasion of starting to piece together the fact that songs could have meaning beyond 'Boy meets girl, and then they dance'. Songs conveyed meaning; they carried stories; referred to important issues; underlined emotional impact; soundtracked personal, emotional, political and symbolic worlds.

Meanwhile, Radio Hauraki released a compilation album called *Homegrown*, which celebrated new, independent local music. Local music on radio was, and remains, something of a contentious issue in broadcast music radio the world over, but it has a particular resonance in New Zealand because of some unique characteristics of the popular music industries and the dominance of Anglo-American popular music in a primarily English-speaking, post-colonial nation. Importantly, the radio station not only recorded and released independent local music, it actually playlisted those tracks on air, and (naturally) the more I heard them, the more of a fan I was of those artists and those songs. Partially as a result of that short and rather unusual episode in New Zealand radio history, it has always seemed to me self-evident that radio stations can play songs to make them popular – not simply because they're popular. Something that was great, influential and powerful about that Homegrown album, of course, was the idea that, in order to be a musician – or to put out a record – you didn't have to be as international and enigmatic as David Bowie, nor as glamorous and funky as Donna Summer. Not that New Zealand records hadn't existed before 1980 – just that I'd never really noticed that they were New Zealand records. Jon Stevens, Mark Williams, Sharon O'Neill and Split Enz were just pop stars, and so separate from my reality that their New Zealandness pretty much entirely escaped me until my early teens. There was local music, of course – but then there was radio music. Music has always been centrally important to me, and radio was the method through which I arrived at my appreciation for music of all stripes. British listeners had John Peel. We had Barry Jenkin: Doctor Rock.

In 1981 – just a couple of years after it originally debuted on BBC radio in the UK – *The Hitchhiker's Guide to the Galaxy* was broadcast on the National Programme via the YA stations around the country (1YA in Auckland). And my cassette recorder was put to good use making sure I didn't miss a moment of it. Not just for me, but for my generation of radio, storytelling and comedy enthusiasts, Douglas Adams had created a masterpiece of its medium. And, while the story is still broadly revered, it's often forgotten that this was a radio programme that only later became a series of books, a television series, and a feature film. For me, though, almost better than the radio series were the records that used essentially the same scripts, almost all of the same actors, most of the same sound effects, and (it seemed) just a little more care and attention when it came to the direction and sound design. *The Hitchhiker's Guide* was radio for the airwaves, and then it was radio for release on records. This slight mutation in mediation factored in the realities of its context. It was considered in terms of its medium-appropriateness and specificity, which, as will become apparent, is something I deem to be a tremendously important consideration, to the extent that the translation from one medium to another is something that I believe *The Hitchhiker's Guide* did more successfully than anything that came before it, and more than most of what has come since. Again, you'll bear in mind that this is an entirely personal perspective, and not in any way a statement of fact. I listened to those records and my cassettes of the radio series so often, I can still, to this day, recite the first half-hour episode verbatim, from memory, start to finish. The theme tune to *The Hitchhiker's Guide* still sends shivers up my spine whenever I hear it.

I guess it was unsurprising, then, that I ended up in radio. In fact, long before radio initiated my academic career, it first ruined it. Rather than attend my undergraduate classes in English literature, art history and music theory at the University of Auckland, I went straight up to student radio station bFM and tried to find ways in which I could be involved. I could think of no finer reason to be in an institute of higher education than to sit in a studio, play records and talk into a microphone.

I will spare you the detail of my progression through student radio, to an unpaid apprenticeship in the studios at 91FM and Radio Hauraki; of my helping set up the short-lived (and almost comically doomed) Manukau City radio station Oasis 94FM; bluffing my way into a job making ads for Radio Pacific for about five years; researching, writing and producing my first radio documentary series in 1994 (a 26-part, 1-hour a week programme about the history of jazz that nearly killed me); set-ting up my own radio production company making radio drama series, jazz programmes and other syndicated shows; hosting a nationwide specialist music radio show; creating children's radio programmes; making documentaries; starting the NZ Radio email discussion list; instigating the Auckland Society of Low Power FM Broadcasters; and lobbying for a New Zealand children's radio station. But I'm not going to do that, because I'm not writing my memoirs here, and the point of this story has been made, I think.

And that point is this: I love radio. Radio is, in large measure, who I am.

It's important – both to me personally and, more significantly, for a proper understanding of this book – that you realise the full meaning of that fact, because without really understanding how significant radio is as a defining cultural force and as a central part of my life – not just of my career – I think what I have to say would probably have a good deal less impact, and less significance. In fact there'd almost be very little point in me saying it, and almost nothing at stake.

But even more consequential than the enthusiasm I have for the medium and its legacy is the caveat I mentioned right at the outset: I am putting my hand up to admit to a degree of advocacy for radio, as well as to being immersed within both the fandom and the professional practice cultures of radio broadcasting. As a result, my understandings of the medium are coloured by an immersion that necessarily sets some factors as 'common sense' or as 'what is obvious', and, while I will endeavour to make strange some of these very familiar concepts and taken-for-granted premises so that we will be able to distance ourselves from them and critically observe them in as objective a manner as we can, there will, I expect, be some traces of essentialism, some residue of that immersion and some unavoidable perception bias within the work. My ambition, however, is to declare this potential problem upfront and to alert you to its possibility, so that you will be able to identify that phenomenon not only within this text, but also within other texts in the radio studies tradition.

Where to Start

One of the problems one often experiences with any analysis of radio as a broad subject area – and perhaps this problem can be said to exist across the entire body of academic work known as the field of radio studies – is an underlying assumption about an agreement concerning what is meant by the word 'radio' itself. If one looks through the literature of the field or peruses back issues of *The Radio Journal*, topics such as government broadcasting policy, industrial practice, documentary programme making, music programming, representation and identity, community and the public sphere, textual analysis and technical management of the electromagnetic spectrum all feature. While these topics may be broadly related and connected by the idea of a shared (though contested) understanding of what radio is as a cultural institution and technological form, that idea perpetually sidesteps the question of definition. And while, in the main, definitions are problematic, leading one perhaps to conclude that the best course of action would ordinarily be to work from this assumed (albeit vaguely stated) starting point, there is now the problem of a shifting context. In a larger and broadly static media environment that includes a range of electric media forms (television, the telephone, recorded music, and so on), some lack of clarity about the edges of radio is tolerable, because as an object of study, radio tends to hold still as we examine a particular component. However, as part of a changing media environment, radio becomes a moving target. The edges blur – and so it begins to seem more important to ascertain (or at least attempt to clarify) exactly what is and what isn't radio. Something is happening to radio – indeed something has happened to radio – and in order for us to understand what has changed about it and what that means, we need to stop and attempt to gain some clarity about what 'radio' was in the first place. And it is, I would assert, only when one attempts to step outside of one's own experience of, advocacy for, and immersion within a particular manifestation of that media form that it is possible to identify and dispassionately track changes in its technological and societal context. This book is an attempt to achieve that goal, and my own personal frame is something that I rely on you, the reader, to help me keep out of this work. I am not the subject of this book. None of us is. And, more importantly, I plan to argue that none of the things we hold dear and like to call radio is what is at stake within this work. As uncomfortable and counter-intuitive as this may appear, what we like to think of as radio is not radio. In fact, in a very important sense, radio may not, in fact, even exist.

Kate Lacey (2008: 22) has already posited this provocative thought:

> there is no such thing as 'radio', and yet there is still valuable work for radio studies to do. Or to put it another way, it is the

very idea of radio with which radio studies need to engage to connect with debates beyond the confines of radio studies.

The idea of radio being a non-existent medium may seem, at face value, patently absurd, but it is no more absurd than the idea that what we personally have experienced as radio is what radio is, in any meaningful form. Lacey's assertion that we need to explore radio's 'porous and shifting boundaries' is well made, and it is taken very seriously within the context of this book. But, all the same, an analysis of radio in the digital age appears to demand, at the very least, a clear starting point. We understand that the phenomenon we refer to as radio is clearly not restricted to one's own, personal experience of radio. It is clear that radio is an entity that can remain consistent enough to be discussed as a discrete object of analysis that shifts between media environments, much as a dumpling with porous edges may be transferred from one soup to another and remain a dumpling. And so we remain confronted with the question: What, in fact, is radio?

Essentialism and Epistemology

A book entitled *Understanding Radio* (Crisell 1986) seems a sensible place to start looking for our answers. It opens with the following assertion: 'What strikes everyone, broadcasters and listeners alike, as significant about radio is that it is a blind medium.' Crisell goes on to explain that he means we can only hear rather than see its messages – and not (of course) that the medium itself cannot see. But, leaving aside the question of 'blindness' for a moment, consider instead the totalising 'what strikes everyone'.

In fact radio is such a different experience for people – at different times, within different contexts, and depending on what it is they are actually paying attention to – that 'what strikes them' may in fact vary greatly. What appears to be significant to the individual observer of radio is not universally shared. Both ontologically and phenomenologically, radio is a complex and multifaceted entity and set of experiences. An assumption of a universally shared impression of radio seems to me to be a deeply problematic place to begin. However, the greater problem is one of essentialism, and it is one that I go to great lengths to avoid (if not entirely erase) in this book.

Radio need not necessarily mean a particular type of audio content consisting of some combination of speech, music and sound effects, coming from a particular type of device. That is common, perhaps, but it is not an essential characteristic of the medium. Other authors have ventured that the central or defining characteristic of radio is that it's personal – or that it's a secondary medium, which is to say we don't so much listen to it as have it on while we do other things. Berland (1990) notes this apparently commonly agreed characteristic and identifies it as having developed as a commercial strategy rather than as an inherent quality of the medium:

> Radio is commonly referred to as a 'secondary medium' in the broadcasting industry. The phrase conveys the industry's pragmatic view that no one cares whether you listen to radio so long as you do not turn it off.

And, while it is easy enough to find this philosophy repeated in the corridors of certain types of radio stations by certain types – or pay grades – of staff members (assuming that they are situated within a particular political economic context, at particular periods in recent history, in a specific cultural or geographic territory), you will not have to look hard to find someone who will assert the opposite. Radio is just as likely to be 'compelling' as it is to be 'wallpaper'. The condition of 'secondariness' is not a prerequisite for a medium, phenomenon or practice to be considered radio. It's perhaps a useful and descriptive idea in some instances that have been selected for examination and analysis, but it is far from being an essential characteristic; nor is it by any means always true of every experience or instance of radio.

The epistemology of radio is therefore an interesting territory to explore: that is, what do we actually know about radio, how is that knowledge acquired and to what extent can we really understand it as a medium? It's easy enough to coin (and uncritically repeat) these pithy 'radio is . . .' phrases – and they can be useful in the sense that, intuitively, people often do know what you're talking about. However, it is also the case that what we mean when we say 'radio' is often left unclear, or is the subject of assumption. We may be referring to radio as an institution; or as a method of transmission; or as a professional practice; or as waves in the electromagnetic spectrum; or as a physical item that sits on the kitchen bench or car dashboard; or as a type of programme that one happens to be listening to.

Radio consists of shows, stations, schedules, studios, managers, sales reps, presenters, producers and technicians. It includes and connects with political economies, legislation, a broad range of technologies, the physical properties of radiation in the electromagnetic spectrum (and our ability to harness those waveforms), promotional cultures, music industry integration, local and regional as well as national characteristics and manifestations, brands, celebrities, real people's lives (audiences, interviewees and radio workers alike) and – importantly – other media. It is different in different places, at different times, and within different contexts. More importantly, it is often different from one instance to another, even within the precise same geographic locale, legal framework, political climate and period in history.

What strikes this author about radio is not its blindness, but rather its connection with people's lives, with history, with technological development, with jobs that people do in the industry, with programmes: drama, music, documentary, magazine, commentary, news, entertainment and other genres – with popular culture and with a shared understanding of our society and how it works. And, importantly, those things – all of those things – change over time and in response to environmental, cultural, technological, legislative and social shifts.

And yet not one of those things is essential to radio. Radio can exist without music. It can exist in a completely different legislative environment. It can (and does) exist without the use of radio waves. It can exist outside of the context of brands and stations. It need be neither personal nor secondary. These might be commonplace conventions, but they are not necessary characteristics in order for what we call 'radio' to be radio.

David Black (2001: 398) encounters this problem in his analysis of internet radio and comes to the perhaps inevitable conclusion that radio is best defined simply as that which people agree to call radio:

> Listeners have a lot to do with it. A medium's identity stems in part from how it is received and treated by its users. Listeners may of course be nudged in this or that direction by the industry. But if, for whatever reason, Internet audio is treated as if it were radio, then to some irreducible extent it is radio.

Stephen Lax (2011: 152) points to the problem of measurement within this shifting environment. In order for it to be ascertained how many people are listening to radio via digital means, an agreement must first be reached as to what is considered to fall within the realm of radio and what is considered to fall outside of it:

> [The CEG] recommended that 'digital listening' in this instance should mean listening to DAB radio, rather than including all digital platforms. This would compare like with like since DAB, as a terrestrial broadcast system, was a direct replacement for FM radio. Like FM, therefore, it was portable, whereas listening through a television or on the Internet was a different kind of experience, and did not incorporate the essence of radio, its mobility. Research conducted for the BBC Trust supported the importance of radio's portability being a key defining characteristic.

The arbitrariness of the decision that, in order to be considered radio, something must first be 'portable' is palpable within the text, but the need to draw lines around a medium in order to develop useful statistics for business intelligence and to inform policy-making speaks to this compulsion to insist on the medium having some essential characteristic, whether that might be portability, secondariness, transmission via electro-magnetic spectrum or, indeed, blindness.

My colleague Tim Wall, currently editor of *The Radio Journal*, navigates this problem of definition by talking about radio as 'a series of discursive practices', which is a suitably vague but generally comprehensive strategy that works as a shorthand to discuss – but not attempt to solve – this complexity; to open up discussion rather than to provide neat answers. I borrow this approach as a leaping-off point towards a richer understanding of radio, so that we may examine the phenomenon and experi-ence of radio in the digital age. However, while I find the notion of media as forms of discourse helpful in terms of its flexibility and a more satisfying alternative to essentialism, I also find myself frustrated by its reluctance to arrive at a conclusion. If radio is, as Black suggests above, whatever people say it is, then theoretically radio can be almost anything. My contention is that radio is something specific, but that its specificity is to be located by examining the consistencies that are present within those changing discursive practices that surround it, rather than by declaring it to have some essential characteristics on the one hand, and by allowing any interpretation as acceptable ('if that's what you want to call radio, then fine') on the other.

My aim in this book is to examine the nature of these discur-sive practices and find common threads as well as consistent and coherent ways of talking about what radio is and what it means, so that we may have some clarity and agreement – if not in fact certainty – about what radio is. In so doing, it will be possible to analyse and draw conclusions about the ways in which this medium, its manifestations, and the discourse that surrounds it have changed or have different meanings in a media environ-ment characterised by a predominance of 'digital' technology rather than by a predominance of 'electric' technology.

This is what I mean by the title of this book. It is not about the digitalisation of radio broadcasting or about the development of digital broadcasting platforms, though of course those will be important issues to discuss as part of this narrative. Nor is it about podcasting, online music services, timeshifting, or iPods, though – again – these are both relevant and interesting. This is not a book about digital radio.

This book is about radio – and everything radio means – in an age that is characterised by digital media. There are some entirely analogue radio practices and forms that persist in the digital age, and these are as worthy of our attention as those that employ new and cutting-edge technologies. So in order to attempt an analysis of radio in the digital age, it is important at least to attempt to arrive first at some clarity, if not fixed definitions, about what is meant by those terms: 'radio' and 'digital age'.

Discursive Categorisation

As I have mentioned above, the phenomenon that we call radio changes from place to place, in different legislative and cultural contexts, as well as over time. So to draw a direct line from the early development of the point-to-point 'wireless telegraphy' experiments of Marconi to contemporary DAB broadcasts, podcasting, mp3 streams and Last.fm requires a number of quite significant imaginative leaps. In order to be able to claim continuity of any kind, it would seem that a technologically deterministic narrative that posits strong cause and effect between different developmental eras of radio is necessary – and, while these connections are often assumed (unstated, but present) as direct causal linkages within the body of radio studies literature, this is not necessarily a desirable or a helpful conclusion to reach. However, neither is an argument in favour of distinctive breaks, in which technologies are 'revolutionised' at significant points of innovation throughout the medium's history. This discontinuity theory of media development usually favours a narrative that highlights a particular agency, often that of a great person or 'genius' who discovers, invents or reconstitutes the medium in some new form. In fact the reality is necessarily more complex, and a comparison between the phenomena of radio at different points in history (for example, 1927, 1967 and 2007) must factor in the observation that, even at a specific given point in time (say, in 1927), radio existed in different forms, in different places, to serve different needs, and for different political, social, economic and cultural reasons.

In an attempt to solve this dilemma – the fact that we can neither claim continuity nor distinctive breaks – I propose that radio does not actually have any essential characteristics – not even that it favours audio over visual communication. And, while it is likely that most forms of radio that we will ever encounter probably will have a primarily audio media aspect, there are other communicative media forms that we do not call radio but that also prioritise audio content (CDs, iPods, telephones, remote doorbells, bluetooth headsets . . .). So, instead of looking for characteristics that persist regardless of radio's form, historical period, geography, purpose or context, I suggest that there are categories of characteristics that we can use to speak about radio across all of those different milieux, and that these categorical frames remain useful despite the changes that may occur in any aspect of radio.

To that end, I have identified the following ten categories of discursive frame that appear to remain constant throughout the development of radio over time. There may be others, and indeed readers may wish to construct their own systems of categorisation using these ten as a starting point. However, I find the following divisions useful, and I offer this method of partitioning the discourse in the hope that it contributes to a useful and workable approach to an analysis of the medium in a changing technological environment.

Device There is a physical, tangible form – a machine, if you will – that we call 'a radio'. It might be on the kitchen bench, in the car dashboard, part of a home stereo system, built into (or coded as software within) a mobile phone or laptop computer, and so on. The physical manifestation of the radio device is significant: it is not just that through which we listen but, in many ways, it is itself the thing we are listening to. A focus on the radio device draws our attention to the properties and characteristics of the medium through which our own experience of radio takes place.

Transmission Whether electromagnetic radio waves at varying wavelengths modulated by amplitude or frequency, wired internet connection, cellular mobile communication, satellite or some other method of distribution, the means by which radio content reaches our devices is an important component of a complete discussion about radio. Changes in the means of transmission affect (and are affected by) all of the other categories of radio discourse here.

Text We speak of radio texts, which may be programmes, of course; but, as a discursive category, they also include all of the formats: shows, advertisements, dramas, documentaries, podcasts, voicebreaks, playlists, songs and so on.

Subtext This is created by the meanings and intentions of the texts – including the underlying purposes for making radio (e.g. Reithian principles, commercial endeavours) – which shape the way in which radio is manifest. We may also experience the subtexts of radio as metanarratives.

Audience While this is a particularly problematic term (especially in the digital environment, where the boundary between producer and consumer can often be blurred), much discourse of radio surrounds the people who 'consume' the text – whether they are co-creators and participants in the construction of the text or simply passive recipients, in groups or individually.

Station While the idea of a 'station' might impose a particular model of professional practice and institutional form on the discourse of radio, we may use the term more broadly, to refer to the organisational framework in the context of which radio texts are instigated and produced.

Political economy It is important to consider the legislative framework, political environment and economic forces that shape the medium, as well as the ways in which radio generates capital or performs some social or civic function.

Production technologies These are the tools used to create radio texts. Production technologies may include the microphones, mixing consoles, tape machines – or indeed the 'smartphones' – on which programmes and programme segments are produced.

Professional practice This discursive category is closely related to the production technologies and will often describe their being operated by the people who perform what constitutes 'radio work', whether through employment, hobby or voluntary engagement. However, many of the practices that go to make up radio work may not actually relate to the use of radio production technologies (for instance, radio sales).

Promotional culture This discursive category deals with the ways in which radio connects with and contributes to knowledge of and participation in other activities, products and services. This includes music business integration, public service announcements, author interviews and so on. The promotional culture of radio is inevitably linked with the texts and subtexts of radio, but it warrants a separate analytical frame to draw attention to the effect (and intended effect) on the consumer behaviour of audiences.

Categories as Analytical Frames

These ten categories or discursive frames provide a means through which an analysis of radio can be approached. It is important to underline, once again, that the items that fall within these categories are subject to change in different places, times, contexts and technological environments and that no combination of their manifestation is essential at any one place or time.

In one city, at one point in history, different manifestations of radio may coexist that may share none of the qualities within any of the categories, and yet they may all equally be considered radio. It is for this reason that reductive and essentialist definitions of radio are problematic. While of course not all things are radio, neither is there one characteristic or set of parameters that all manifestations of radio must share in order to be described as belonging to the discursive terrain we collectively refer to as 'radio'.

The purpose of the ten categories above is therefore to offer a frame through which a discussion of changes to radio might be essayed. In other words, radio has always been multifaceted, complex and diverse. But now it has become many new and different kinds of multifaceted, complex and diverse. Where there is essentially no such single thing as radio, establishing the effects that shifts in technological, political, social, cultural and economic climates have had on the medium is deeply problematic. But, with the aid of these categories, there is at least a way to have this conversation without first proving able to nail down what radio was before it changed and what it has become in the process. In other words, radio has no fixed, essential characteristics, but its characteristics can always be discussed in terms of the analytical framework that the categories provide.

Techne and Time

When one considers the media environment within which radio operates, the conceptual approach of radio as a 'technology' seems a very limited part of the story and an incomplete frame through which to analyse shifts in the ontological and discursive nature of the medium. While the changes may seem primarily technological in nature, more is in fact changing than just the machinery and tools through which radio is made manifest. Although the age that we are interested in here is 'digital' in nature, clearly it is not simply the case that the tools are digital, nor is it obvious that the technologies are themselves the sole leaders of change within that digital environment. Here I follow McLuhan and Zingrone (1995) and employ 'techne' – from the Greek noun *technē*, ancient and modern – to suggest not merely technologies, but also techniques and, importantly, the craft and aesthetics of radio. My understanding of the common, contemporary usage of the word technē in modern Greek is that it is often used as a synonym for 'art'. I believe that to borrow the term *technē* and to fold this combination of the three core concepts of tools, techniques and art into one indivisible concept provides for us here a useful paradigm. The three are essentially inseparable, and hence to talk about shifts in techne over time rather than just about shifts in technologies gives a richer, more nuanced picture of the nature of the changes that we seek to understand.

Of course, the inter-relationships between these three separate concepts are easy to see: the professional practices that take place with respect to the medium of radio are related directly to the technological environment within which they are situated; the kinds of programmes and approaches that may be possible or desirable are suited to the tools that enable them to happen; techniques and tools are developed in response to innovation in aesthetic forms and in order to solve problems and challenges raised by inventive radio producers, who push at the edges of what is currently possible through existing processes and devices. But that these three inter-related concepts of tools, techniques and craft should be considered to form a singular phenomenon provides, I believe, a clear and useful framework for understanding the nature of the media ages that we migrate between. There are obvious continuities between the different eras, but the techne of the electric age of radio differs in very large measure from the techne of the digital age of radio – to the extent that there is, in fact, a distinctive break between them – and we can therefore examine the latter as a phenomenon in its own right, while observing and respecting those continuities. Grouping these interwoven aspects into one core concept provides us with a good method of preventing an artificial prioritisation or attribution of causal power to a single aspect that undergoes translation over time. Technology may differ; but, if process and craft remain constant, what has changed? New methodologies may arise; but, if the tools used and the end result arrived at are identical to what has been arrived at before, where is the significance? But, as techne alters, the changes to what we call radio become both stark and profound.

The continuities and breaks within the techne of radio praxis reveal themselves through what might appear to be mundane distinctions. Radio producers use tape, or they use digital editors; technicians may have broadcast engineering or software development roles; presenters may sit in airconditioned studios or in their bedroom at home. There are what we might consider to be 'traditional' radio jobs: sound engineer, presenter, producer, copywriter, traffic scheduler, music programmer, station manager – and so on . . . but even within what might be thought of as traditional broadcast radio paradigms, the day-to-day activities of the people who perform those roles are very different today from what they were even 20 years ago. This does not refer just to the tools they use (many of which are virtually unrecognisable from one era to the next); but even the functions and actions they perform and the outputs they generate are often radically altered.

However, it's important to bear in mind, when comparing the technological infrastructure of a radio station of 20 years ago with that of a station of today, that the transition was a gradual one, with intervening and transitional technologies that came at different periods, many of them being adopted and then abandoned by these radio organisations. A wide variety of digital and analogue digital hybrid tools have appeared and disappeared as innovations have taken place, been adopted or discarded, improved upon or supplanted by superior (or cheaper) tools. Frequently an item that may have been thought of as an industry standard or even as cutting edge barely a decade ago – even fully digital tools that may at first have cost tens of thousands of dollars – may be considered positively quaint today. And, with the passing of these interim technologies, many tool-specific practices and workflows also disappear.

For instance, in the late 1990s and early 2000s, the DAT (digital audio tape) machine was a piece of audio recording and playback equipment that very few professional radio studios would be without. Commercials were mastered to small DAT cassettes, as were pre-recorded programmes and other programme features. While these tiny tapes may not have had the convenience of the continuous loop tape cartridges ('carts') that had been ubiquitous in on-air and production studios for nearly 50 years prior to that and continued to hang around well into the last part of the twentieth century as a testament to that convenience (though not necessarily to its reliability), they scored over the larger, more fussy medium of reel-to-reel 1/4" tape in terms of storage capacity, access speed and signal-to-noise ratio.

Likewise, during this period, data storage devices were a lot larger and contained substantially less information than the much smaller hard drives and solid-state storage devices – like USB memory sticks – do today. When I worked as a production engineer at Auckland's Radio Pacific around 1995, radio commercials were transferred from production studio to on-air facility on Bernoulli hard drives – a now largely forgotten storage medium that resembled large floppy drives, approximately 14 cm x 14 cm in area and about 9 mm thick. These removable drives had storage capacity of 90 MB, 150MB or 230 MB and cost hundreds of dollars each. Today a typical SD card can contain about 100 times as much information for not much more than the cost of a cup of coffee, and a pocket-sized external 1 TB hard drive retails for less than US$100.

Kryder's Law (similar to, and often confused with, Moore's Law about computer processing power) suggests that hard drive storage cost per unit of information halves about every 18 months to two years, though the rate of progression has had several significant leaps in the past decade due to breakthrough advances in storage media and the utilisation of error-correcting codes. However, rather than simply upgrade storage media every few years to keep pace with the rate of technological change, radio stations have had to make decisions about what technologies to adopt and what workflow practices those technologies suggest or enable. For instance, because of the internet data traffic speeds available in 1995 (and the less than widespread nature of internet connectivity at the time), the Bernoulli drives used by Radio Pacific, which contained the day's commercial production work, were collected and delivered by courier each day.

The commercials of that radio station at that time were shaped by a range of influences, including that of production and distribution processes and practices, as well as of the technologies used to create the advertisements themselves: the word processors used to create the copy; the compact disc music libraries from which music beds were selected; the microphones and processing units in the studio; the means by which commercials were scheduled, catalogued, stored, replicated and broadcast – and so on. In addition, the specific human craft that combines words, sound effects and music in different ways for the purpose of entertaining, persuading and communicating – a craft created within a particular set of socio-cultural environmental parameters, both in the workplace itself and in the context of a particular demographic of New Zealand society, which made up the intended audience for that communication – all contributed to the final form and expression of these advertisements.

Techne provides a way for us to consider collectively these different parameters – and for us to witness and reflect upon change over time. It is this concept that I will use to group together the phenomenon of radio praxis and the related epiphenomena. If we do this, we can explore the periodisation of media history without quite so many loose ends lying around. This allows us to identify and explore the nature of the digital media environment more readily – the context of contemporary techne within which the discursive practices of radio are now situated.

CHAPTER TWO

Radio in the Digital Landscape

Periodising Media History

If one accepts that the phenomenon of radio, as understood through the categories described in the previous chapter, is a complex and discursive practice situated within a political, geographical and cultural framework, it is reasonable then also to agree that radio 'in the digital age' is just as complex and multifaceted as it was in the 'pre-digital' era – but that it differs mostly in that it is contextualised within a technological environment characterised by digital media forms and communications media. In other words, this book considers the 'age' as the thing that is digital, rather than the medium itself. Shifting the emphasis from the object to its context allows for a broad range of complexities, continuities and discontinuities. Most analyses of radio in the digital era have focused specifically on the digitalisation of transmission methodologies or the digitisation of the broadcast content (for instance, Lax 2011, O'Neill 2008, Rudin 2006, Dunaway 2000, Black 2001); or they have centred on the application of what might traditionally be thought of as 'radio' programming and production techniques to digital media forms that are not always considered to be 'radio' in any conventional sense (for example, Berry 2006).

In contrast, one of the central premises of this book is the notion that studying radio in the digital age does not preclude a study of analogue radio forms and technologies (nor of pre-digital radio practices); however, those analogue forms and processes are now situated alongside and within digital forms, in complex and intertwined arrangements, and in consequence ratios shift and behaviours alter, as do the meanings, uses, gratifications, functions, phenomenological experience and ontological status of radio. Simply put, we are interested here in an analysis of what radio is and how we understand it from our viewpoint here, in the digital age. Hence our focus is not so much on specific events, inventions, interventions, policy developments, acts of individual broadcasters or consumer electronics manufacturers; it is not even on establishing (or attempting to establish) a 'history of the future' of radio broadcasting. Instead this book explores the metanarrative of media ecology, and it does so in search of an understanding of radio within a digital context. And while specific events, broadcasts, individuals and programmes will be held up for examination along the way, these are intended as case studies, to illuminate a broader set of processes rather than to function as discrete objects of analysis from which universal principles can be established. They are symptoms, certainly, but not, in themselves, diagnoses.

For this reason, the present chapter examines instead the ways in which the digital age can be understood as a discrete period of media history, both from a technological perspective and from a cultural perspective. Ideas from the field of media ecology help illuminate the notion of digitalisation and the effect of a changed, digital environment on the media we use. I also borrow the concept of 'affordances' from psychology (Gibson 1977), and particularly its use within an ontological framework (Sanders 1997), which shows us how environments (specifically, for our purposes, media environments) can be understood as spaces in which certain opportunities are available for an actor within that space. As that environment changes (from an analogue context to a digital one), those affordances alter, and different opportunities become available as others become less accessible. In addition, I am interested here in the ways in which the relationships between people traditionally thought of as 'producers' and people thought of as 'consumers' of content are transformed within that environment. I propose a holistic approach to radio studies; one that is interested in connections between seemingly

disparate phenomena, accepts a multiplicity of seemingly contradictory factors, and prioritises an understanding of the broader
contemporary noosphere – Pierre Teilhard de Chardin's (1955)
useful term for the technological, cultural, political, social and
intellectual ecosystem that connects, contains, shapes, informs
– but, importantly, is also created by – the sum of human
activity.

I propose that contemporary 'radio' is digital in much the same
way in which the radio of the twentieth century was 'electric'.
That is, it not only used that particular 'flavour' of technology,
but also followed the conventions and practices inscribed by the
media environment within which the discursive practice took
place. We will explore the transformative nature of digitalisation,
including its potential for the addition of multimedia elements
to traditional audio-only aspects of radio broadcasting, as well as
the ways in which the digital context affords different approaches
to radio as a medium, a professional context and a consumption
practice.

Ages of Media

To speak of an 'age' is to define and historicise a period that
is characterised by a dominant aspect – specifically, I would
assert, a dominant technological or media aspect of that era. The
ancient Greek poet Hesiod is credited with an attempt to divide
history into metallic ages. His formulation attempted to explain
how mankind came to need to work. On the basis of the idea
that the iron age was preceded by a bronze age, he postulated a
theoretical golden and silver age of prehistory. The first race of
men was golden (the most precious of the known metals); it lived
without labour because the earth produced food spontaneously.
The metallic raw material of each age was the 'medium' in which
crafts, arts and cultural expression (once again, techne) were
represented and preserved and the tools of day-to-day life were
articulated. Since, he reasoned, iron was cheaper than bronze
and the age of bronze had preceded that of iron, those very few

more valuable metals must surely have preceded that one in turn. In other words, there must have been a hypothetical gold age and a silver age, which led inevitably to the bronze and iron ages of which Hesiod had knowledge. We know, of course, that no such ages actually existed, but this core idea was subsequently addressed in different ways by Greek and Roman poets and so the notion of a 'golden age' has persisted as a metaphor that has been utilised in other contexts to refer to a time when things were better – before things were debased and degraded. Lucretius later developed this model and presented it not as degradation, but as a form of cultural evolutionary progress that marked those periods of history when humankind put more abundant and replicable media forms to use in the service of their arts, culture and sciences. The idea of increasing abundance and replicability of media is an important one in the narrative of media evolution, and it is one we shall return to.

Following C. J. Thomsen's classification – in his 1836 *Guide to Northern Antiquity* (published in English in 1848) – of archaeological finds into different categories on the basis of the typology and chronology of objects found, archaeologists and paleo-anthropologists now use a 'three-age system' (Stone Age, Bronze Age and Iron Age) to denote the phases of human intellectual and cultural development according to the primacy of the technologies, raw materials and tools used for the creation of each society's cultural artefacts (see Malina and Vašíček 1990, Barham and Mitchell 2008, Lubbock 1865, Gräslund 1987, Heizer 1962). These ages are further subdivided: the Stone Age into paleolithic, mesolithic and neolithic; the Bronze Age into copper and bronze. These ages describe not only aspects of the activities and objects of the people who lived in them, but also the kinds of economy, social structure, political infrastructure and religion of the time. That is to say, the primary medium of the age provided the context within which the unique nature, institutions and conceptual framework of the humans who lived in that time emerged. In other words, human civilisation is the text of that mediation. As Paul D. Miller evocatively puts it:

> Stop. Think about it. Every sensation you have comes from one
> source: civilization. When you finish this paragraph, put down
> the book for a little while and look around you – check out your
> surroundings. What can you see, hear, smell, taste, that does
> not originate in or is not mediated by civilized people? (Miller
> 2008: 6–7)

This idea of civilisation as context of mediation has been
expressed by a number of scholars over time, but perhaps most
notably by Lewis Mumford, whose *Technics and Civilisation*
(1934) posits technologies as both defining and being defined
by the prevailing characteristics of the culture of their time, and
especially by the sophistication and intellectual and practical
developments of that time. Echoing Thomsen's prehistoric categorisation, Mumford divides civilisation since medieval times
into an eotechnic, a paleotechnic and a neotechnic age.

Similarly (and with a great debt to Mumford), McLuhan
(1962) demarcates several different periods of cultural history,
according to the dominant forms of media and communication. However, in so doing, he leaves archaeology behind and
abandons the physical raw materials (stone, iron, bronze) from
which bygone cultures have been constructed, favouring instead
the predominant communicative form as the central defining
characteristic of an age of civilisation. McLuhan offers speech
and writing as two significant early ages of humankind. As a
species, he asserts, we had an 'oral age', followed by a 'scribal
age'. The discursive medium defines the civilisation and the
historical period in which we live. While the things we make out
of iron or stone might well be expressions of ourselves and our
culture, nothing defines who we are and expresses us better than
the primary method through which we communicate with our
contemporaries (rather than with future archaeologists). In *The
Gutenberg Galaxy* (1962), McLuhan links the interiorisation of a
new technology with the translation of culture from one form to
another.

Significantly predating McLuhan, as Crook (1999: 12) has
observed, British broadcaster and author Hilda Matheson (1933)

has not only – similarly – demarcated these cultural translations and contextualised them as media shifts, but also raised questions as to their effect:

> The history of mankind down to our own day might be shown, as Mr H. G. Wells has suggested, in five different stages: (1) Before Speech, (2) Speech, (3) Writing, (4) Print, (5) Mechanical Transport and Electrical Communication . . . How can we escape from this new noise that is adding to the distractions of an already complex world? Is it to be yet another by-product of man's inventive mind which will get beyond his control before he has learnt its power? (Crook 1999: 13)

Further, that translation of culture is not simply a shift in what we do and make as a species, but (quite literally) a transformation in who we are as a species. Communication forms are, to McLuhan, media technologies. Speech and writing are technologies of communication and, as such, they are extensions of ourselves. The adoption of a new technological framework of the media alters ratios between our senses: the means by which we take in information about the world and form understandings of it. By changing the nature of our technologies, we change the nature of ourselves.

> My suggestion is that cultural ecology has a reasonably stable base in the human sensorium, and that any extension of the sensorium by technological dilation has a quite appreciable effect in setting up new ratios or proportions among all the senses. Languages being that form of technology constituted by dilation or uttering (outering) of all of our senses at once, are themselves immediately subject to the impact or intrusion of any mechanically extended sense. (McLuhan 1962: 35)

Thus McLuhan not only posits media as environmental in nature, but also goes further to assert that for us they are essentially the only environment that genuinely matters, as they profoundly impact upon what we can say, how we can understand, and the ways in which we can perceive (compare Miller's point above). While an overly literal reading of this conclusion would find a disturbingly strong deterministic narrative in which technology drives history and media would be something that 'happens to us', in fact we would do well not to overlook the first part of McLuhan's famous aphorism: 'We shape our tools, and then they, in turn, shape us.' That is: we shape our tools.

(Those interested in the origins, filiation and history of ideas may wish to stop for a second and take stock of the following comment, which can be found at http://mcluhangalaxy. wordpress.com/2013/04/01/we-shape-our-tools-and-thereafter-our-tools-shape-us/: 'The quote "We become what we behold. We shape our tools and then our tools shape us" is often mistakenly attributed to Marshall McLuhan. It does NOT appear in 'Understanding Media', as Wilson Miner confidently asserts in the presentation below, indeed it does not appear in any published work by McLuhan at all. The quote was actually written by Father John Culkin, SJ, a Professor of Communication at Fordham University in New York and friend of McLuhan. But though the quote is Culkin's, I would argue that the idea is McLuhan's, as it comes up in an article by Culkin about McLuhan: Culkin, J. M. (1967, March 18). A schoolman's guide to Marshall McLuhan. *Saturday Review*, pp. 51–3, 71–2. The idea presented in the quote is entirely consistent with McLuhan's thinking on technology in general.' The author of this blog post is Dr Alex Kuskis.)

Ala-Fossi and Stavitsky (2003: 65) remind us of Jock Given's (1998) provocation that digital communication technologies 'do not get invented in laboratories or backyards removed from social, economic, and political processes as pure technological determinism would have us to believe' (28). But these tools are not neutral. In fact the dominant technologies of our times (print, electric, digital) define our age in at least as significant a way as stone, bronze and iron have defined the ages that came before ours. And, given this fact, we have unarguably shifted from an age characterised by electric and electromagnetic technologies (recordings and broadcasting, for the most part) to an age characterised by digital technologies. In so doing, we have shifted from an age of somewhat abundant 'mass' media – though with finitudes and scarcities (such as spectrum availability) – to one in which we have discovered ways to put ever more abundant and replicable media forms to use in the service of the arts, culture and the sciences – and, simply, to express ourselves to other human beings.

Hesiod, I think, would be satisfied with this.

The Ontology of Media Affordances

The difference between the view held by strong technological determinists – who assert that media make us do certain things and be in certain ways – and the (surely more palatable) view of media ecology – through the frame of 'affordances', which allow for human agency within an altered techno-social framework – is a hugely significant one when one examines media under the process of profound technological change. In the case of radio in the digital age, the former position follows the essentialist line of some thinkers alluded to in the previous chapter, who assert that radio simply is a certain way (personal, secondary, portable, time-bound, blind and so on) and merely translates that into a new context, which seems simply to be another way (asynchronous, global, abundant, democratised, online, visualised and so on). This line of thought leads us into certain avoidable traps: first, that radio is necessarily a particular way in the digital age (and therefore uniformly a particular way in the digital age); and second that digitalisation is an external force that happens to an industry – to be resisted by that industry, to be welcomed by that industry as a challenge to the status quo, or to eradicate that industry altogether. There is a good deal of rhetoric about digital technologies causing 'the death of' all sorts of things – radio included – and similarly a lot of rhetoric about the triumph of radio in an age of increasing (mostly digital) media competition. But, as Douglas Adams pointed out in his article 'What Have We Got to Lose?' (1998), the question concerning the impact of digital technologies and new media forms on industries such as radio, magazine publishing, and the music business is not that they are problematic simply because we disagree about the effect of that external force:

> [I]t's a hard question to answer because it's based on a faulty model. It's like trying to explain to the Amazon River, the Mississippi, the Congo and the Nile how the coming of the Atlantic Ocean will affect them. The first thing to understand is that river rules will no longer apply. (Adams 1998)

And, while the analogy of rivers meeting the ocean is an admittedly limited one, it paints a vivid picture of the profound recontextualisation of media production, distribution and consumption that the digital age represents. However, it also appears to suggest an engulfing of those industries – overwhelming and effectively erasing their path through the unstoppable force of environmental transformation. This is not, I believe, the case in the context of media shift. My Amazon and Mississippi still have agency. My Congo still has identity – if not as a river, then still as the Congo. My Nile still flows, even though its borders are no longer made of rock, but of more water.

In contrast, Manuel Castells re-frames the debate in a different manner by positioning the technological context not as something that happens to us, but as something that we are, in an ontological sense, or that we are at the very least a part of:

> Our world has been in a process of structural transformation for over two decades. This process is multidimensional, but it is associated with the emergence of a new technological paradigm, based in information and communication technologies, that took shape in the 1970s and diffused unevenly around the world. We know that technology does not determine society: it is society. (Castells 2006: 3)

Echoing Teilhard de Chardin's concept of the noosphere, Castells asserts that we do not simply inhabit but also, importantly, constitute the media environment within which we find ourselves. And, while Castells' point about the unevenness of society and the implications of that inequality is well taken, the underlying prerequisite for his position is that human beings, connected together, are – collectively – the media environment and that the digital tools that facilitate this communication are the points of connection. Communication technologies are not simply tools that are external to us (or forces to be resisted, championed or overwhelmed by us); they are indeed, as McLuhan would have it, extensions of ourselves. Digital media are not something that 'happens to' and transforms our communication – they are how we communicate, or, more precisely, they are us, communicating. Given this fact, it is important to understand what is possible and what is not within that environment. If digital media are extensions of ourselves and not some external force with which we must contend, we are therefore in a position to make decisions about the ways in which we use and express ourselves through these media. That said, our having agency does not suggest that we have complete autonomy. As in any environment, there are rules that stipulate what is possible, what behaviours are to be encouraged (indeed may appear to occur naturally) and what actions are not compatible with the space (or carry with them certain dangers and undesirable outcomes). In other words, the media we create have 'affordances'.

An ontological approach to both the 'affordances' of digital media and our own 'effectivities' (Sanders 1997) provides us with a starting 'world hypothesis' (rather than 'paradigm' – and for the difference here, see Cutting 1982), which guides my view of what is possible – that is, what opportunities and dangers exist – within the digital technological media environment. However, the degrees of subjectivity and objectivity of perception within the media environment are constrained relativistically by the parameters of that environment (in the same way in which Einstein explained movement to be measurable and observable, but only relativistically), and so our ability to observe and consider the ways in which our technological context provides these affordances is impaired (or at least influenced) by our immersion in it. But it is when that environment changes that we have the opportunity to examine, from any 'real' (or at least differently relativistic) perspective, the nature and character of those affordances. This is the position in which we find ourselves now.

As 'an opportunity for action in an environment' (Sanders 1997: 103), an affordance is potential that subsists within a shared context, which may be selected, intended, and acted upon. For instance, if there is a table in the room, an affordance of that environment is that of tabletop dancing. If the room contains no table, there is no tabletop dancing to be done. However, it should be readily apparent that tables do not cause you to dance, and whether or not you do so is up to you. Compared with the media, this example offers a somewhat false analogy, as it suggests a clear distinction between subject and object that is not so readily made in the context of a media environment (especially since, as we have agreed with Castells, McLuhan and Teilhard de Chardin, the environment consists of extensions of our own selves). Nonetheless, environments have affordances and it should be clear that affordances of the digital media environment differ from those of the electric media environment.

Strong technological determinism would have us attribute causation and, strangely, intention – as in 'information wants to be free' – to what is (from an essentialist perspective on media) an external, inanimate and mechanistic other, with fixed and non-negotiable properties. On the other hand, a view of media ecology that understands the noosphere in terms of affordances and our participation – as media creators, participants and consumers (as well as, let's not forget, as technologists and inventors of tools within that media space) – in terms of effectivities with respect to those affordances restores that agency to the people who operate in, communicate through, and themselves make up that techno-social environment. This seems a more convincing, and – importantly – a more useful position, which promises to yield rich and nuanced insights into technological shift rather than simplistic and reductive bumper sticker slogans. It is, then, from this perspective – one that acknowledges a wider societal shift, which is neither particular to radio nor significantly different, for that medium, from what it is for any other human activity that operates within (or under the influence of) a digital environment – it is from this perspective that I intend to examine radio in the digital age.

The 'Characteristics' of Digital Media

It is difficult (to say the least), not to mention somewhat arbitrary, to put a date on the shift from the electric age to the digital age. The first record to be released on compact disc (CD: the first digital consumer music format) was Billy Joel's '52nd Street', in October 1982. But the Radio Computing Systems 'Selector' digital music programming software was being introduced to radio stations as early as 1979 – and computers for billing and even scheduling were not unusual (if not exactly common) prior to this date.

To understand the influence of this shift upon the medium of radio, it is necessary first to explore and make sense of digital media themselves. Here I make an important distinction between the 'electric age / digital age' binary on the one hand and the 'analogue media / digital media' binary on the other. It so happens that electric age media are typically analogue in nature (though there are exceptions), but the choice of distinction is important in defining digital media in terms of their key ontological differences, which in turn provide them with their affordances for radio (and other human communication forms).

Radio is, broadly speaking, a sound medium, and sound is analogue by nature. As a function of the movement of air caused by vibration, the voice of a radio announcer is, by definition, an analogue phenomenon. Likewise, the music emanating from radio speakers or headphones and entering the ears can only be analogue for the simple reason that numeric data are not an audible phenomenon unless converted into an analogue form (sound waves). Moreover, even the transmission of digital signals is primarily an analogue event. The electromagnetic spectrum that carries the voices and sounds of radio from a broadcaster to its audience is a series of waves of different lengths and frequencies. A wave is continuous and flowing, while digital media are discrete, separate. So to talk of digital audio and digital radio is necessarily to speak of a process of translation.

The conversion of information to digital formats and the ability to compress that digitised information to a size that can be easily accommodated by transmission systems form the central enabling technology for new methods of broadcasting that are being increasingly implemented around the world. Digitisation converts information processes from traditional electronic and analogue forms of any kind into a series of 'ones' and 'zeros' that can be manipulated mathematically by any computerised device. Converting audio into data involves sampling the audio in regular and rapidly occurring 'snapshots' in order that an analogue waveform can be represented as points on a line, described by a sequence of ones and zeros. Perhaps the most important characteristic of digitalisation is that it converts the core information of the communicative process into a single, indivisible unit: the binary digit, or 'bit'. In his book *Being Digital* (1995), Nicholas Negroponte compared the atom – as a core, indivisible unit of physical matter – to the bit – a core, indivisible unit of digital information. In a digital media environment, all information – whether it be the recipe for Coca-Cola, the photograph of a suspected terrorist, the collected works of Geoffrey Chaucer, a season of *Breaking Bad* on DVD, a database of the Automobile Association members' contact information, a hit song by Rihanna, a British Rail timetable, or a collection of topographical maps of the Galapagos Islands – exists in the same easily stored, easily manipulated, instantly duplicated and readily distributable format. Paul Levinson notes:

> Prior to digital computers, the encoded form differed from medium to medium; for example, grooves in a record were incommensurate with patterns of electricity in phone wires, etc. The digital improvement in this regard, then, was to make the encoding process the same for all media. (Levinson 1999: 165)

Another key difference between analogue media and digital media is that analogue media consist of continuous waves, while digital media are discrete. Wikipedia, the online open source encyclopedia, observes:

> Digital refers to the property of dealing with the discrete values rather than a continuous spectrum of values ... The word comes from the same source as the word digit: the Latin word for finger ... as these are used for discrete counting. (Wikipedia 2004)

While an analogue medium such as AM (amplitude moderation) or a vinyl record has characteristics about it that introduce noise to the signal (interference in the case of analogue broadcasting – surface noise and scratches in the case of records), it is at least a representation of the same kind. Sound, which uses waves caused by vibrations, is stored and conveyed in a homologous (though not identical) manner across formats. Digital formats concerned with the storage and distribution of audio, while often cleaner sounding, are, by definition, approximations of waves. Instead of following a continuous line, as a wave does, a digital audio signal is made of (abstractions of) points along that line – points described in ones and zeros. It may be a very accurate approximation, but it is an approximation (and compression) nevertheless, and it is fundamentally different in character from the analogue properties of sound, though the perceptibility to humans of that difference is debatable.

While it might seem odd to consider radio to be akin to a visual medium, McLuhan conceptualises it as such. Like a book, radio is a 'hot' medium that emphasises the same sequential linearity that print offers. Just as words are such that we read them one after another in a linear sequence, radio is, to McLuhan, a linear, time-bound medium. Traditionally speaking (and with the necessary cautions about essentialism), listening to a radio broadcast tends to happen in 'real time', and the running order and progression of that broadcast's content are both dictated by the originator of the programme and identical for all recipients, simultaneously. However, paradoxically, radio also figures within the electric age, which McLuhan characterises as having acoustic properties: by this he means a surrounding, 'all at once' characteristic. But the acoustic properties of the electric age are acoustic in the same way in which a sermon from a pulpit is acoustic. It is simultaneously received and it constitutes an immersive experience, but it has no conversational properties.

Digital communication, on the other hand, exhibits characteristics that can be described as having more acoustic (or rather 'acoustic-ish') properties akin to the tribal campfire storytelling that both McLuhan (1964) and Walter Ong (1982) refer to: it is 'cool' – non-linear, surrounding (multidirectional) and, importantly, interactive, especially in the sense of being interrogable and interruptible. One of the key tendencies of digital media is the potential for the disruption of the content's relationship to time and geography. They are innately decentering. Digital media are non-linear and are not locked in sequence to chronological time. Any medium (in the case of our analysis, radio) that has been translated to the digital environment is thus subject to an enhancement or amendment of its auditory (acoustic-ish) characteristics – or at least its affordances in this respect. Manuel Castells argues that the nature of temporality under conditions of new (digital) media is at once 'simultaneity and timelessness' (Castells 1996: 491) – the very opposite of the broadcast radio that McLuhan describes as 'hot', which is of a sequential and time-bound nature. Once again, this is not a 'characteristic' of digital radio forms in the sense of being prescriptive, but rather a set of potentialities afforded to these forms by the technological context. Digital is an inherently multimodal media form: you can use the environment to create or emulate acoustic or visual style communication experiences. But its affordances provide a much greater scope for radio to take on these interrogable 'acoustic' properties than the previous technological context did. Indeed the extent to which that is made possible has a potentially radicalising effect on the medium of radio.

However, it is important to note that McLuhan allows for – in fact prescribes – this radical transformation of media characteristics under conditions of environmental change. McLuhan and McLuhan's *Laws of Media: The New Science* (1988) attempts to locate the forces of media translation within a framework of scientific laws that can be used to establish the 'effect' of that shift. To the McLuhans, any new medium has particular kinds of interconnected influences on the prevailing media ecology as a whole, and that medium can be interrogated and analysed in a systematic and reliable fashion using the *Laws of Media*. These laws take the form of four questions that can be applied to any technology in order to examine the environmental effect it has as a medium. As noted above, for McLuhan, all human tools are media, since they all extend some aspect or characteristic of the user. The wheel is an extension of the foot, the gun an extension of the fist, and so on (see also McLuhan 1970: 54).

The four questions are:

(1)   What does any artefact enlarge or enhance?
(2)   What does it erode or make obsolete?
(3)   What does it retrieve that had earlier obsolesced?
(4)   What does it reverse or flip into when pushed to the limits of its potential (chiasmus)? (McLuhan and McLuhan 1988: 7, slightly modified)

Thus, using McLuhan's tetradic 'laws of media' framework, the process of digitalisation could be said to enhance radio's acoustic nature, render obsolent its print-like linearity, retrieve the surrounding, 'all at once' immersive nature of the tribal campfire and reverse to a time-independent and geographically unconstrained screen-based media form, which exhibits few (if any) of radio's earlier characteristics. Note, however, that we have no difficulty in distinguishing 'radio' from 'not-radio' in our day-to-day experiences of everything, from streamed audio on a laptop to DAB receivers with rewind buttons. After digitalisation, the relationship to earlier analogue forms is so distant that the use of the term 'radio' to describe the new medium is called into question, as discussed above – though, as was also noted, radio's condition as a discursive practice rather than as an essentialist form (and the categories I have proposed in chapter 1) allows us to incorporate digitalised radio into our conception of radio as a whole.

The Ecology of Tele-Information Services

According to Bordewijk and van Kaam (2002), there are four main communication modes of 'tele-information services':

- ALLOCUTION: the supply of information outwards from a central point. Allocutionary media can be considered 'push' technologies, as they send material chosen by the provider outward, to passive recipients. Broadcast media are considered allocutionary in form.
- CONSULTATION: the supply of information on request from a central server. These media forms may be considered 'pull' technologies, as they release centrally held material as and when chosen by the recipient. Consulting a directory, phoning a lawyer or accessing a library may be considered examples of consultation media forms.
- REGISTRATION: the supply of information by a user of the information service and not by the service itself, but under the programmatic control of that information service centre. Examples include sites that allow users to build their own profiles within strict parameters. YouTube, news agencies, and online multiplayer gaming platforms provide examples of this.
- CONVERSATION: the sharing of information between the tele-information service's consumers, under the programmatic control of the consumers themselves. Conversational media may be thought of as contexts for communication rather than sources of communication. Examples include telephones and Twitter conversation.

Further, these four modes can be broadly divided into two subsections, depending on where the information originates.

Allocution and consultation media depend on information supplied by the service itself; registration and conversation depend on information supplied by the users of that service, or 'user-generated content' (UGC). Of these four, allocution is that which is most like what we understand as 'broadcasting', in the way radio has traditionally been configured. But this is not the only, nor indeed the historically inevitable manifestation of communication using the technologies provided. Electric era radio technologies afford more possible configurations of service provision than simply one-to-many broadcast models, and Citizen Band (CB) radio provides us with an example of a conversational implementation. Likewise, it has been noted by some scholars and practitioners alike that radio has always been interactive and that there have been elements of user-generated content within the context of radio programmes such as phone-ins, request shows and segments containing listener voice contributions.

Putting aside these examples, which are fairly marginal within the grand scheme of dominant worldwide forms within the twentieth century, radio has arrived, however, at an allocutionary dominance as a result of a series of agreements; a set of power relationships (primarily those of business and political interests); a collection of technological developments and innovations within that context; and a range of other historical, cultural and societal factors. The electric era technological context provided a range of affordances negotiated by a complex interplay of human agency and techne, such that we have arrived at what we call 'broadcast radio' as a normative construct – albeit one with many variations, manifestations and exceptions. Radio audiences have, of course, been able to select from a menu of stations until now, but in the digital age the media environment is radically different, and for that reason the set of affordances provided by that context is also profoundly different and the resulting normative construct (to the extent that one can be observed) is also categorically changed.

Once again, power relationships, innovation, and other influences of human agency, individual and corporate, come into play to make use of those affordances; but, while the conventions of what we have come to call 'radio' factor large within that negotiation, the parameters of all of these ingredients have altered, and the discursive practice of radio is reshaped in response to these forces. As a result, allocution (or 'broadcasting') is not necessarily the dominant form of radio in this changed environment – or, if it is, it is at least significantly less so – and it is of value to pay attention to the ways in which other models of tele-information service architecture are being implemented (or may be implemented) for radio in the digital age. There are continuities, and it is important to recognise them, but the disruptions are remarkable.

Similarly, the differences in power relationships, the innovations, and the socio-political environmental factors that shape the media environment are all of interest here, and I note below just a few of the ones that contribute to the ways in which radio is manifest in the current context. It would appear that an effect of the changed media environment has not been to supplant one tele-information infrastructure with another – but instead to move from the context of a single dominant mode to a multivarious environment, within which allocution, consultation, registration and conversation are more equally weighted.

Technologies of Interaction and Decentralisation

One innovation that has contributed greatly to the dissemination of digital media – and particularly that of audio files – is data compression. By removing elements of redundancy in a digital file and by sacrificing comparatively small amounts of audio fidelity, file sizes can be dramatically reduced. By making file sizes smaller, data can be stored more efficiently and more information can be transmitted in a more reliable fashion over transmission media limited by bandwidth. This core technological development has made digital broadcasting not merely possible, but viable. But it has also contributed to a range of affordances for other tele-informational architectures. The development of an ability for programming to be archived and made available 'on demand' (consultation), for instance, is made possible – or at least more technically and economically feasible – through the reduction of file sizes for storage and distribution. The capacity for hard drive data storage has increased year on year, with diminishing costs, allowing for an exponential expansion of the ability for content providers such as broadcasters to automate the archiving and retrieval of any form of time-based content – thus releasing the content from the confines of 'time of broadcast'. Digital media are also endlessly replicable. A data file can be perfectly duplicated without degradation (theoretically) an infinite number of times, and distributed or given away. There is no limitation of supply and no loss of quality. Each copied instance of that file is in all possible ways equivalent with its original. By removing elements of scarcity, this phenomenon impacts upon the economic basis for media production and distribution.

At the same time, however, issues of ownership over media content and over the components of that content (for instance songs within radio shows) provide an example of power relationships and tensions that may restrict certain implementations of a consultation approach to digital era manifestations of radio. The struggle over intellectual property is far from the only restrictive force upon radio innovation, however. Ala-Fossi and Stavitsky (2003) observe that there has long been a tradition of suppression of radical potential in this area.

> American inventor Edwin H. Armstrong developed FM technology in the 1930s, but this static-free system, with sound quality superior to AM's, was seen as a threat to existing AM markets of commercial network radio, as well as to RCA's patent monopoly for AM technology and AT&T's program distribution business. Further, FM technology would have required people to buy new radio receivers – while for RCA it was more important to get them to buy television sets (Winston 1998, Douglas 1999, Walker 2001 Hazlett, 2001). (Ala-Fossi and Stavitsky 2003: 74)

This suppression of innovation by incumbents, then, is nothing new and we should not be surprised when it happens within any changing technological environment. But incumbents can also be sites of innovation, and in the UK the BBC is a good example of a major broadcasting organisation with a mandate for innovation, although this innovation takes place primarily within an allocutionary framework.

Examples of interactivity in the context of radio are easily located within allocutionary radio broadcasting. And, while these forms of interactivity do not necessarily shape the overall output of the programme in terms of its form, structure, direction or intent, there is at least a contribution made by the listener to the communication that is taking place. That is to say, while the extent of the interactivity may be questionable and the conditions and context for it contestable, the fact of it is fairly undeniable.

Online there are increased opportunities for radio station listeners to engage with the institution and potentially become part of the programming output of the station. Online chat rooms offer listeners a side channel to the broadcast programming (for instance, the IRC channel of BBC Radio 1's weekday evening programme hosted by Zane Lowe). Not only can listeners contribute their thoughts, in the hope that their submissions might be incorporated into the programme content, but they can also interact directly with other listeners within the online space, as well as with programme producers and station staff members who are monitoring and moderating the message board. This takes the traditional broadcaster further from the phone-in or write-in request (or indeed from the text-messaged comment) and more towards its developing a potential for genuine influence over the programme output.

Tom Robinson's BBC 6 Music radio show *Now Playing* is all but programmed by the listeners, who contribute links and suggestions for music tracks to play, offer contextualising comment and interact live with the programme using social media platforms. The production and distribution of the programme takes place in a fairly traditional, centralised fashion, but the degree of interactivity (that is, the listeners' ability actually to determine aspects of the programme's output) is somewhat higher than in many other programmes. However, in many respects, the programme could be said to occupy a similar space to that of phone-in (or, even more accurately, write-in) request programmes, in which a music radio show is constructed from listener song suggestions and the accompanying narrative. That is, the programme is built by the broadcaster according to broadcasting standards and conventional practices, by mining from a body of material submitted by the station's or the programme's listeners.

A wide range of forces and interests, both seemingly emancipatory and restrictive, shape the media environment. Within that context, the media forms that emerge do so as a creative response from individuals and groups. The ultimate form of the medium is socially negotiated. However, what is significant here for radio as a discursive practice is that, while the affordances shift from one media environment to another, the practices and cultures of radio production, distribution and consumption are not uniform, nor have they ever been. Exceptions outnumber norms, and it has always been like this. Widespread and sustained listening to a range of different types of radio stations and radio-like services across genres, in different countries, at different times of day and in different historical periods brings up a fascinating, complex and diverse array of discursive practices. What is interesting for our purposes and will be explored in later chapters is the extent to which we can make observations and draw conclusions about the digital media environment from instances of these practices that appear to be significant or provide useful case studies.

We do not seek a general theory of radio in the digital age, but rather a series of special theories that are consistent with each other, with the media environment and with our experience and observations of the medium. In so doing, we may come to understand the digital age through the lens of radio far more than the other way round (as one might expect).

CHAPTER THREE

Radio and Everyday Life

Within the allocutionary, electric age context, radio marks out the ordinary day-to-day lifeworlds of its listeners in a number of different ways, not the least of which is through the division of broadcast programming into schedules that include 'breakfast' programmes and 'drive time' shows. Of course, the connection with the lived experience of time runs much deeper than this, and this complexity is explored in the literature. Rather than simply reflect daily life, radio both performs and shapes it through the features, spoken word, routines, music choices and regular segments that makes up its content. Paddy Scannell has written at length about the relationship between broadcast radio and that routine of lived experience (1988, 1996); but, rather than merely observe the influence of radio listening on the patterns and routines of ordinary life, Scannell is especially interested in the perception of time and the social psychology of media with respect to circadian rhythms and temporality. He asks: 'Would time feel different for us without radio, television and newspapers?' (Scannell 1996: 149); and he proposes that indeed it would. My follow-up question in this new context would be: 'In what ways does time feels different for us in the context of those media forms here in the digital age, in comparison to how it felt when the original question was first put?' In other words: 'Is it, in the digital age, a different kind of difference from the one Scannell witnessed in the electric age?'

Of course, in many ways, everyday life in the digital age bears a great deal of similarity to everyday life in the ages that preceded it. People still get up in the morning, they eat their breakfast, they go to work, they relax, do chores, enjoy sport, play with their children, go shopping, talk with their friends, cook meals, take care of their pets and go to bed at night. Nobody's routine is identical, of course, though most could be said to be similarly 'ordinary' in many respects. However, in many ways, that routine is also very (even profoundly) different, simply because of the media environment within which those activities take place. Work, for instance, is radically transformed by digital media technologies. The commute to a place of employment is, for many people, a fundamentally different experience with the addition of laptops, e-book readers, smartphones and portable music players. Many of the day-to-day shopping activities that traditionally took place in a high street, a mall or a supermarket might now take place at home or in a café, in greatly different circumstances and often at very different times of the day. Leisure activities are scheduled differently; they are organised by using social media platforms, SMS, VoIP, software such as Skype, and email; and they can even take place within an online rather than a physical context. Some of those 'virtual' activities are often ones that in a previous media age would have been quite unthinkable: the rise of massively multiplayer online campaign gaming is just one very popular example.

In addition, the dominance of scheduled programming is challenged in an age of on-demand listening, and the ability to select live radio alternatives that originate in entirely different time zones or are comprised of music scheduled entirely independently of any reference to events, the passing of time or any other information that would distinguish a particular day from any other makes a significant difference, which alters radio's relationship to daily life. When Scannell (1996: 151) asserted that 'the situational properties of broadcasting always attend to time', it was almost certainly not clear that this was neither a permanent nor a necessary characteristic of broadcast media, but simply one that pertained primarily to the media age within which he was at the time situated. The age in which the fact that broadcast time maps directly onto experienced time could be said to be an essential property of radio is well and truly over.

That is not to proclaim the death of anything – least of all of live radio – but rather to highlight once again a series of developing complexities; to demonstrate the range of different affordances provided by the new media environment; to subvert the temptation to essentialism; and to warn us away from the lure of seemingly obvious, simple answers. In fact the place and role of radio as part of daily life within that altered media context, when accorded careful analysis, reveals an incredibly complex relationship, full of exceptions and conditions. It is no longer enough (if it ever was) to simply assert, for instance, that a certain proportion of listening happens in cars, or that the market research for a particular breakfast show demonstrates patterns of listenership that suggest a massed routine activity such as waking up and starting the day during a specific quarter-hour period.

Ken Garner observed that radio's real text is the clock on the studio wall (1990: 194) and noted a continuity of format and delivery in popular breakfast radio throughout its history. Indeed his observation, over 20 years ago, that networked British breakfast radio will invariably serve up a 'golden oldie' at 7:30 a.m. – and had done so since the 1970s – can still be relied upon today (at least on the FM band), as my own listening has evidenced.

> When is the listener's need for reassurance greatest, but after the news? Without exception, every surveyed edition of Tarrant, Mayo and Marshall broadcast a golden oldie after the 7.30 a.m. headlines. (Garner 1990: 200)

However, the affordances of the digital environment in which radio is now situated disrupts and in many cases entirely sever, both the seemingly necessary connection between live transmission and reception and the notion of a shared, simultaneous community media experience. No longer can 7:30 a.m. be relied upon to be experienced at 7:30 a.m., nor will a song follow a news bulletin, nor will 8:00 a.m. occur half an hour later, at 8:30 a.m. In other words, not only will the time of broadcast not necessarily match the time of reception any longer, but the order of the programming content and its nature constructed in the form of a 'show' might well be reconfigured and given a new meaning in the experienced lifeworlds of its audience. Indeed, rather than imparting a sense of getting up and getting on with the business of the day, the affordances of digital media consumption mean that audience members can choose to repurpose the radio content so as to make it reinforce and accompany their own schedules, whatever they may be. While digital technologies may not have freed us from the shackles of the calendar or liberated us from the tyranny of circadian rhythms, they may well have loosened the ropes somewhat, so that we may have a bit of space to roam, both temporally and psycho-socially.

I examine the phenomenon of timeshifting (and the case of podcasting) as just one instance of the effect of the production, distribution and reception methodologies that digital technologies offer and of the consumption practices they enable. As a result of the affordances of these new technologies – and of the manner in which, and extent to which, those affordances are utilised – the social and cultural meanings that may be derived from the timeshifted media texts alter. Of course, digitalisation also significantly impacts on the daily routine of radio workers, as technologies such as digital syndication, ISDN, voice-tracking and digital studio recording, and editing practices provide a context for significant changes in the everyday practices of what we might term 'radio people'; hence this is explored here in order to illuminate the extent of the changes rather than to make any attempt to catalogue the effects of those changes to the technological environment comprehensively.

Digital technologies have also, arguably, eroded the differences traditionally experienced between 'metropolitan' radio stations and their regional and small-town counterparts. While in many countries local and national radio stations have long existed side by side (the UK is a good example here), there are many places around the world in which the existence of a nationally networked commercial music radio station is a relatively recent phenomenon, and one that has come about as a result of the networking potential of digital media forms – both in and of themselves and as agents of connection between more technologies of analogue transmission. In these circumstances, the daily life that is reflected by radio is arguably more generic and detached from localism and locale – or, at the very least, it reconfigures the relationship between temporality and rural space, to make that temporality align more closely with urban time. And because, like the medium of radio, daily life is itself immersed in the digital media environment, the representations and mediation of that daily life contain much that reflects the digital environment: the things that we find to be invisible, unremarkable or mundane parts of our surroundings and day-to-day lives, but that exist only because of the affordances of digital techne, have necessarily become the content of the text of radio broadcasting as well.

Time and Timeshifting

One of the most commonly observed challenges to the orthodoxy of broadcast radio introduced by digital techne is the way in which the latter offers alternative approaches to the experience of programming with respect to time. There are three primary aspects to this phenomenon. The first is that audiences may choose to listen to a programme when it is convenient to them; to 'listen again', as it were. The second aspect, related to the first but significant enough to be considered as a separate effect, is that the programme does not necessarily continue irrespective of the listener's activity. It can be made to pause, skipped ahead or back, and resumed at any time. Not only can an audience member reschedule the radio station's output at his or her whim, but the manner in which that listening takes place is more akin to reading a book: by picking it up and putting it down again as the mood strikes rather than by stepping into a continuously flowing stream, which carries on, oblivious to whether the listener is within earshot or not. The third aspect is that programming, once liberated from schedules and timeslots, may be re-edited into packages and segments or enhanced with additional material that may not have fit into the original broadcast timeslot. The atomic unit of online radio content is, then, not necessarily the programme (which can often run to three or four hours) but individual segments, interviews, and features – sometimes just a few minutes in duration.

There are several significant implications of these three phenomena of digital timeshifting that are important to radio both as an institution and set of professional practices and in terms of its consumption cultural practices. The first of these implications is that listening takes on more of a selective, deliberate quality. Rather than tuning in and passively consuming whatever happens to be on, listeners may select from a vast menu and actively choose what is of greatest interest to them. Of popular broadcast radio, Berland (1990: 179) notes that 'its primary goal is to accompany us through breakfast, work and travel without stimulating either too much attention or any thought of turning it off'. But timeshifted radio cannot rely upon the 'safety of the bland' in the way traditional broadcast radio often does, as its criterion for selection is primarily 'interestingness' (and, perhaps secondarily, duration – on which more below). The tension that arises from the fact that a large proportion of on-demand radio programming starts out as broadcast programming leads us to an interesting situation, where there may be a tipping point at which the observation of Berland may no longer hold. As timeshifted listening becomes more prevalent and more central to the outputs and activities of radio institutions, the characteristics of programmes that are successful in an on-demand context may conceivably become more sought after and prioritised by producers than those characteristics that are considered to be successful in a broadcast context. In other words, in the digital age, interestingness may trump aural wallpaper as a deliberate programming strategy.

However, it is important to note that these methods of delivery, with their complementary (rather than contradictory) relationships to temporality, are not mutually exclusive propositions. In fact the reverse appears to be true. People do not seem to be choosing on-demand listening options instead of broadcast programming, but rather to be choosing from among them in a manner that is suitable for a particular purpose or context. While it's true that audiences cannot add to their listening indefinitely and without limit (simply because of the number of hours in a day), and certainly nobody is likely to listen to more than one programme at a time, it's also true that timeshifted listening does not, strictly speaking, replace traditional time-bound radio programming. Instead there is a shifting of ratios as the new media practices are adopted.

At a time in which people can – and many do – timeshift a proportion of their radio listening, traditionally scheduled, linear and time-bound radio broadcasting seems to be as popular as ever in most marketplaces around the world. Listenership surveys, such as RAJAR in the UK or Arbitron in the United States, clearly point to a majority of the population choosing to tune into live broadcast radio in a way that suggests that 'Radio' (capitalised here to denote the institutional form as it is traditionally understood: as an allocutionary, broadcast medium with its associated conventions and characteristics of 'liveness') is seemingly under no threat whatsoever as a cultural phenomenon. However, a closer inspection of these surveys and of the marketing materials that the radio industry generates by using their results suggests that there is some significant diminution of consumption, but that it is not measured by the number of people tuning in (cumulative audience), but rather by the time they spend listening. On-demand listening competes for attention with live listening, but, rather than stealing audiences, it is – perhaps appropriately – competing for time.

Garner observed a phenomenon that appears to remain true to this day, for this generation, and for perhaps precisely the same reasons:

> Breakfast radio thus appears to be retaining its popularity . . . because it is indelibly associated with the act of getting up and going to work or having to busy oneself about the house. (Garner 1990: 195)

That is, the fact of that listening seems not to have significantly changed; but the context in which it happens and the fact that the duration of the listening appears to have been compressed to accommodate changes in social and cultural practices as well as the practice of timeshifted radio content (and a whole range of other media forms that compete for attention) are entirely significant. But, while there could be said to be erosion of time spent listening – both to live radio and to radio as a whole, as media consumption becomes more strategic and audiences gain greater control over the times, places and manners in which they consume radio content – there is also an upside for the industry, as Stiernstedt observes:

> The temporal, as well as the spatial control over the audience has, from a production perspective, become harder to achieve through tools like schedules, flow management and formats. Conversely, new media technology creates new possibilities of monitoring the audience, which goes far beyond previous methods of generating survey data. (Stiernstedt 2008: 117)

Quantifying the audience is something that is of primary importance to the traditional radio industry, and yet it is an activity that has eluded it – at least quantifying with any degree of accuracy has – because of the technical and experiential challenges of measuring the extent to which people are listening to live broadcast radio at any given time. Even the act of switching an FM radio receiver onto a particular station is no guarantee that the listener is within earshot of that radio as he or she busies him- or herself around the house getting ready for the day. And even counting each instance of that receiver being turned on is close to impossible in the electric media context, relying on sampled, aggregated and fairly inaccurate diary-keeping survey methodologies. Capturing and quantifying precise data regarding listenership is simpler (and has a much finer degree of granularity) with digital, on-demand listening. So a trade-off for the industry might conceivably be a reduction in numbers in exchange for an increase in the ability to count them.

The practice of timeshifting radio listening takes a number of different forms, although – significantly – they all shift the mode of tele-information service in Bordewijk and van Kaam's (2002) model from one of allocution to that of consultation. Rather than simply put out a single, fixed, linear, time-bound broadcast that listeners can choose to tune into or not, the radio station or institution also becomes a database of audio programming that listeners can select as from a library and consume at a time and in a fashion that suits them.

One disruptive model related to (but not merely an instance of) timeshifting is the relatively recent phenomenon of podcasting, which not only alters the relationship of radio consumption to temporality, but also provides new ways in which that programming is distributed; alters the relationship between the radio programme maker and the audience (from 'tuning in' to 'subscribing'); changes the work routine of the programme producer; and raises interesting challenges to the discourse of radio making as a purely professional set of practices.

Podcasting

Menduni (2007) discusses podcasting – a term coined by *Guardian* journalist Ben Hammersley (as explained in Berry 2006) – as part of a history of social practices of personal, portable music consumption and its experiential effect: that of a private sphere within a public space – Flichy's (1991) 'communicational bubble' – originating with portable gramophones in the 1920s, continuing with the development of transistor radios and earphones in the 1950s, and advancing with the introduction of the Sony Walkman in the late 1970s. In so doing, he raises some interesting observations about the potential for podcasting as a niche consumption activity for the 'prosumer flâneur' rather than as a democratising force of media propagation. As digital techne, the podcast could therefore be interpreted as a fairly minor event in the continuity of technological mediation of private listening. However, the conflation of the phenomenon of the podcast with social and private consumption of music is limited in a number of ways. It overlooks much that both broadcast radio and online audio media owe to speech: that the consumption of speech programming is experientially and psychologically different from private music listening, which is often of an immersive nature; that podcasting as a prosumer activity involves not only the consumption but also the production of radiophonic works for distribution; and more. As a result, the podcast falls outside the continuity of music consumption practices and warrants investigation as a phenomenon that perhaps shares several characteristics with other discursive areas of analysis, including personal music listening, allocutionary broadcast media production practices, online streaming of audio content and the mp3 as an audio media format. Given these characteristics, 'podcasting' as a phenomenon of production, distribution and consumption cultures and technologies is discussed in different ways throughout the course of this book. However, the key innovation of podcasting, at least as developed by Dave Winer and Adam Curry, is the method of distributing digital media files as enclosures within RSS ('Rich Site Summary' or, popularly, 'Really Simple Syndication') feeds. There are plenty of examples of downloadable audio media files online (and these existed well before the birth of podcasting). Amateur radio production predates podcasting, as does private listening on portable devices. What is different here is the degree and sophistication of automated delivery of stored media files. It is as a means of distribution that podcasting becomes most interesting for our purposes, because it provides a distinctive break from earlier methods of audio (and, later, video) content and breaks radio programming, whether professional or amateur, away from the four-part Bordewijk and van Kamm model and from the simple allocution/consultation dichotomy, which had been the frameworks of previous online radio forms. Without going too deeply into the specific technical implementation of RSS technologies, the fundamental principle is that, rather than having to visit a website regularly to see if it has updated content, an individual can use an online or software feed reader to receive new information automatically, via an Extensible Markup Language (XML) document, as it becomes available. The innovation of adding an enclosed media file within that XML document allows for the file to be automatically retrieved by subscription.

With respect to the lived experience of podcast subscribers (for instance, as they commute to work), this distribution methodology facilitates a kind of experience that goes beyond 'on demand', but in fact allows for a new type of schedule setting. A stock of stored audio content is available to the listener: it was automatically downloaded as a result of some previously made choices and is ready to play. The audience member is then able to negotiate his or her own routines – that is, those that work for his or her lifestyle, activities and movements. Someone's train journey to the city centre might be regularly accompanied by a podcast of WNYC's Radiolab; a Saturday morning cup of coffee might be routinely enjoyed with BBC Radio 4's Friday Night Comedy; and so on. Often listeners will match the duration of podcast to the duration of activity. A reader poll of preferred podcast durations conducted by blogger Richard Farrar (2009) suggests that periods of 30 minutes or less are a more convenient duration for listeners, even if traditional radio programmes might not fit into that same time frame. One explanation for this preference is that this length of time fits with the typical duration of a commuting journey for many listeners, and another is that the convenience of an mp3 download automatically added to a portable media player such as an iPod makes an audio programme of this length a good match between routinised activity, availability of attention, distribution methodology, and reception and consumption technologies at the listener's end.

Like traditional broadcast radio programmes and closely following their model, podcasts that do not originate from radio stations will often adhere to a regular schedule, using the same conceptual model of appointment listening so as to build a regular audience, to fit more effortlessly into its listeners' own routines and to become habitual in that way. Sodajerker on

Songwriting is a podcast in which well-known songwriters are interviewed about their approach to the craft. According to presenter Simon Barber, the show is produced in advance, with sometimes up to four programmes 'in the can', and is typically released on a regular fortnightly (though sometimes weekly) schedule. The programmes consistently range between 45 and 50 minutes in duration and, like a broadcast radio programme, they are released to a fixed schedule. Listeners to that podcast are able to integrate it into their own negotiated listening routines in the same way they might integrate a regular weekly or daily programme that originates as part of an over-the-air broadcast schedule.

That said, many podcasts – especially those from outside of a traditional broadcast environment – may not adhere to a routine at all. For instance, my own New Music Strategies podcast with musician and social media consultant Steve Lawson is recorded and made public entirely as and when it is convenient for us to do so. We meet infrequently, record our conversation on a particular topic, and then upload it to the web. What makes it function specifically as a podcast (in this context) rather than simply as a downloadable piece of audio is the method of distribution: a media enclosure within an RSS feed. Subscribers to the podcast will receive it automatically and listen to it – or not – at their own convenience and discretion. The extent to which that particular podcast (or, indeed, that of the altogether more professional and routinised Sodajerker on Songwriting podcast) is 'radio' in any meaningful sense is another matter entirely – and of course a complex, discursive and contestable matter at that.

Professional Routine

The impact on the lifeworlds of radio listeners is not the only way in which digitalisation changes an experience of radio with respect to time. For the professional broadcaster, the daily work practices are often profoundly different. One place in which this is most obviously manifest is the phenomenon of voice-tracking. The professional radio broadcaster has long been able to pre-record entire programmes to be played back on air at a later time, but these have typically been fully produced and completed programmes. The difference between that and voice-tracking is significant, and the latter is something that can only happen within a digital environment. A programme's presenter can record voicebreaks by using digital recording and playback tools that are integrated with scheduled programming. Those voicebreaks are then played back on air later on, as scheduled, between the appropriate songs or programme features. While the recording of programme segments rather than entire shows may seem like a minor innovation, what it means is that the time taken to actually present a radio programme is condensed, and so the labour required of that broadcaster to complete a radio programme is, at least in theory, significantly reduced. Where a live-to-air programme happens in 'real time', a voice-tracked show can be telescoped into a fraction of that time. Typically the presenter will hear the end of the previous element (the fade-out of a song, perhaps), will record his or her own spoken piece, and then play the next song (and perhaps speak over the instrumental introduction) as if that programme were going live. However, once that voicebreak is recorded, the presenter moves directly to the next voicebreak, hears the end of that song, records the spoken content and continues until the programme is completed, stored and ready to be distributed at a later time. As part of this process of production (and in contrast to live programmes), segments may be re-recorded and transitions between voice and song can be edited. In addition, information from the computerised schedule (including, with a high degree of accuracy, the 'current' time) can be included into the spoken content. With some preparation, an entire three-hour music radio programme can often be voice-tracked in less than half an hour; and, when it goes to air, it presents itself 'as live'.

With respect to the work practices of the broadcaster who now does a three-hour programme in half an hour, this has impli-cations for the workload expected of that employee. They are typically expected to host more broadcast hours of programming, to take on other duties and responsibilities within the station, or simply to work fewer hours for less money. In this way, in the light of these new technologies, economic efficiencies may be made by the radio company – for instance a reduction in the number of staff needed to host the station's output and, in some cases, presenters simultaneously hosting shows on more than one radio station owned by the same company.

The practice of voice-tracking does have implications for the programme's output, of course, and especially with respect to the relationship between the programme and the listener's experience of time. A voice-tracked radio show cannot be responsive to current events in the same way as a live show, nor can it have the same kinds of interactivity that many listeners expect of a broadcast programme. At its simplest, a voice-tracked show can be characterised as following a fairly simple script, in which the presenter names the station, states his or her own name, tells the time, names the previous song played, talks about some songs coming up later in the hour, talks about a promotion currently being run by the radio station, names the song about to be played, and ends with the name of the station again. As a result, this kind of 'That was, this is, you're listening to' form of music radio presentation is one that has a low degree of information content and, to an active listener, a fairly low degree of relevance. Indeed the usefulness of this kind of presentation lies perhaps more in creating the illusion of human company: that there is a speaking voice at all is its value. For this reason, many music radio stations have opted to use voice-tracking for overnight programmes and to keep a live on-air staff for daytime shows. Again, the affordances of digital technology allow for these sorts of decisions to be made. The technologies do not, in themselves, cause radio to become a less 'live' medium than it previously had been.

Another area in which the professional routine of broadcasters is affected by digital technologies and their affordances is that of news and information gathering. Prior to the use of the

World Wide Web as a source of instantly accessible information, radio station newsrooms typically relied heavily upon wire services and feeds from international news agencies such as Reuters and Associated Press. In a local newsroom, journalists would compile stories from those available 'off the wire' and mix them with their own, locally sourced news content. The recording of actuality and soundbites to illustrate a particular news story involved tape recorders, mixing consoles and editing by physically cutting tape content and splicing it together. The same radio station in the digital age tends to rely much more heavily on desktop, laptop and tablet computers, online content, smartphones, portable digital recorders and software editing solutions. The broadcast of the news bulletin itself now has less to do with paper scripts and tape cartridges and tends to use more of an integrated approach, within hybrid software that features scrolling text on a screen for the news presenter to read, recorded segments to be played between scripted sequences, and a process that compiles a news bulletin with a degree of automation previously unavailable. These changes to the ways in which radio station professionals work are not incidental, nor are they simply a response to the technology from station staff members altering their work practices to accommodate the new tools, but they are also actively used as selling features by the companies making this kind of software. For instance, the newsroom software company Burli explains to prospective purchasers:

> It's almost a cliché but it happens to be true: with Burli, your staff can do more than they are doing right now. Burli speeds news production so that your reporters can generate more original stories and spend more time editing and finessing material. (Burli 2012)

The extent to which productivity efficiencies can be made by radio businesses by altering the work practices and day-to-day routines of their employees is not simply an affordance of digital technologies. It is also an opportunity that may be exploited by a newer type of radio business: one that specialises in providing

the kind of station software that makes these sorts of efficiencies possible. At a time when radio broadcasting companies are
perhaps more concerned than ever about profitablity and sus-
tainability in the face of a shifting media environment, greater
competition from other media forms and altering audience
practices, the ability to spend less or extract more labour from
existing human resources becomes a greater priority – and is
more readily achieved.

But making things more efficient by altering work practices is
not the only affordance of digital technologies when it comes to
the day-to-day lives of radio professionals. The practice of engaging in social media environments such as Twitter and Facebook
has become a large part of what radio professionals (and, notably,
radio personalities) do on a daily basis. While there are social and
outside-of-work aspects to many radio broadcasters' social media
presences (offset by the common 'views my own and not those
of my employer' disclaimer in many profiles), the line between
work and not-work often blurs in the online space.

But, as part of the day-to-day routine of programme presenters, the use of social media services as a marketing extension of
their show and of those of their colleagues is a fairly standard
expectation that radio employers have of their staff. An example
of this is the social media activity of BBC Radio 3 presenter
Fiona Talkington, who uses the medium not only to converse
with friends and online contacts (primarily, it must be said,
about music), but also as a promotional vehicle for her radio
programme 'Late Junction':

> Tonight's #LateJunction – Terry Callier, Human League, Sidsel
> Endresen, Kevin Ayers, Inch-Time, Lou Harrison, Kate Rusby@
> BBCRadio3 11pm (Talkington 2012)

Talkington is known as a tastemaker within a particular specialist music niche, and her Twitter followers often have revealed an
interest in the musical discoveries she leads them to outside of
the 'Late Junction' programme. In this respect, the social media
account functions as an extension of her role within the show

and as a way for fans of this area of specialist music to engage with the person who makes these discoveries and recommendations and who reinforces and validates their own tastes and collections. It also offers a seemingly more direct and personal route to connect with her, pass on recommendations and share fan knowledge. As a piece of communication, it appears to fall broadly under the umbrella of working on the show, while often falling outside the time usually allocated to actually broadcasting. The simplicity and portability of social media engagement means that this activity, which functions as professional broadcasting practice (that is, 'work'), will frequently happen outside of work hours. This is by no means a phenomenon restricted to the world of radio, but it is a significant one in this context, as it raises questions about the boundaries between on air and off air, public life and private, employment and personal time – and, in fact, the degree to which radio employers own the labour and output of their staff outside of salaried time.

Updating Facebook pages, sending out Twitter messages and connecting with audiences via a range of digital platforms as part of the daily professional life of the radio presenters and programme makers is a significant shift in their practices and experiences, not simply because these are additional promotional and administrative tasks that add to their workload, but because these activities are, generally speaking, both continuous and incidental. That is, they are not tasks that are given their own time and consideration in the day's workload but must be performed as part of the workday, in parallel with other scheduled activities (for example while one is live on air); and they also extend beyond the parameters of the workday, to the extent that a presenter's social media profile is often also his or her own personal social media profile. The line between work and not-work becomes steadily erased.

For instance, Auckland's Base FM breakfast host Chip Matthews, perhaps knowingly, presents a narrative continuum as part of his Twitter profile. Somewhat like the title characters in Tom Stoppard's 1966 play *Rosencrantz and Guildenstern Are*

Dead, whose activities intersect with their role in Shakespeare's *Hamlet*, Matthews presents himself as a performing member of a professional radio show when he is 'on stage' (on air), but we as audience members and Twitter followers then go with him 'off stage' and witness his thoughts and reflections outside of that context and into his personal life, where he is also a parent, office worker, sports enthusiast and professional musician.

Compare the following tweets – first on air:

> #NP Minnie Ripperton – Young, willing and able, on @BaseFM Breakfast (Matthews 2012d)

> Gig guide, cause we care, and so I can live vicariously through y'all *pause*, on @BaseFM Breakfast (Matthews 2012c)

Then off air:

> Family day out up in whangaparaoa. Mean day. Home, tired. More beer (Matthews 2012b)

> couple hours work left, straight to soundcheck. maybe get a wee dig in too before my gig. jyes [sic] (Matthews 2012a)

Unlike Talkington, whose Twitter stream is largely professional in the sense that her conversations revolve around the music and the social media stream she creates is a clear extension of her public profile and of the show itself, the social media voice of Matthews is that of an everyman who happens to work at a radio station. His Twitter stream provides a glimpse into a private, personal life and rounds out the character within that narrative. This difference between the radio voice and the relaxed, personal mode of Matthews' off-air communication appears to have two key effects: it gives listeners more of a sense of connection with (and perhaps more of an investment in) him as a human being, and at the same time people who connect with Matthews via social media have more of a reminder and incentive to tune into his radio programme.

Base FM is a small, low-power radio station with seemingly very few controls, restraints and enshrined policies about things like the social media activities of station contributors, most of whom are voluntary rather than paid employees. By contrast, at what is perhaps the other end of the professional broadcast radio scale, I conducted some research with Professor Tim Wall into BBC Radio, and in particular into the online activities of specialist music fans and how their online fandom connects with the BBC Radio programmes and stations that play their favourite music. One of the most interesting aspects of that research was the other side of the media relationship: we were given permission to both interview a cross-section of staff and observe the broad range of activities conducted by the broadcast professionals while at work. During the Zane Lowe evening programme on BBC Radio 1, I watched broadcast producers and interactive media assistants do everything from moderate IRC chat rooms, take digital photographs, upload video and audio content, update the website and record a video of guests on the programme (Kele Okereke from the band Bloc Party in this instance). And, while all members of the team demonstrated a degree of engagement with the online aspects of the broadcast, there was also significant separation between the activities of the broadcast team and those of the interactive staff members, and clear power relationships were at work between them:

> Overall, the interactive staff's activities were considered as supplementary and supportive of the primary role. The online component of the show was something to be 'handled' – and while enthusiasm was expressed for the new technologies by all concerned, interactive staff were either performing unwanted but necessary tasks, or running the risk of imposing and getting in the way, as was the case with a handheld video intended for distribution on YouTube and inclusion on the programme's BBC website. The interactive staff member's role was to be as unobtrusive as possible while the production staff, presenter and guest continued making the live radio show. Once the video had been filmed, the interactive staff's role was to edit and post it online as quickly as possible, so that the programme's presenter could include it as part of the text of the show. (Wall and Dubber 2009: 41)

Significantly, the actual level of activity in the online chat room for this very popular music radio show was relatively low, with between just 30 and 40 participants at any one time and, it seemed, no real way to automate the moderation process. In other words, managing the million-strong audience of an allocutionary programme broadcasting live to air appeared to present fewer professional challenges than managing a 40-strong internet forum. The reason for this was, of course, that the BBC people, as publishers, are accountable for the content of all of their media. A one-to-many platform has a single point of failure – one that is professionally conditioned to avoid that kind of failure, and for which there are severe consequences. The many-to-many medium of an online conversational space requires constant moderation if the output is considered the responsibility of the corporation as publisher – and not (or not to the same extent) that of the contributor. Indeed, at one point during the show that I observed, a member of the chat room used broadcast-inappropriate language, and it was some time before the moderator – who was also updating the website live and printing out quotes from the message board to give to Lowe to read out live on air – was able to delete those unauthorised comments. But the benefits of the chat room for the staff we talked to in that instance outweighed the potential hazards. The purpose of using the IRC technology to maintain a live chat room was twofold: that audience members could interact with each other as part of a shared media experience, adding excitement and meaning to the live experience of the programme; and that the content of that conversation could then be repurposed as part of the spoken content of the show, along with the SMS text messages that were also being sent into the programme, selected, printed and presented in much the same way.

It must be said that very few of these ancillary activities about the ways in which Lowe conducted his programme changed very much at all. And, while the music he included in the programme was largely played off the computer and the compact disc (itself a digital medium), for him personally the activity of presenting a radio programme differed very little from the way in which a music radio presenter might have behaved 30 or more years ago. He spoke, he read things from scripts, he pressed the 'Play' button that started the next song, he interacted with his producers, asked what was going on in the news and how that related to the potentially controversial song title of an upcoming track, and so on. But, of course, the professional function of that online engagement goes beyond the creation of programme content; and it alters more about the day-to-day work practices of radio professionals than simply making them engage with audiences in different ways while the programme is going to air. The nature of these sorts of digital media – as countable, discrete and (generally) automatically self-archiving in architecture – means that the broadcaster also has the opportunity to use this interaction between production and consumption activities as an exercise in market research and audience discourse analysis:

> The radio station's websites are, of course, even more essential in this development. It is here, for example, that online communities are created in order to let listeners generate data about themselves through, for instance, talking about various topics in discussion forums, thus generating what one of the programme directors calls a 'self regulating focus group'. (Stiernstedt 2008: 119)

The important point here is that in the digital age even the most traditional and 'electric era' of radio station practices are affected, and the outputs of radio station staff members as well as their routine experiences are profoundly altered by the affordances of digital media. Arguably some of these activities and technologies are exploited for the purposes of profit maximisation and for promotional reasons ('extension of the brand', in BBC parlance); other activities afforded by the digital environment are voluntarily engaged in and positively embraced by station staff members who wish to build a deeper connection with the music and the fans of their programmes and to improve the quality and experience of both the work and the programme output. But, significantly, digital technologies and the work practices they enable, while uniformly profound in their impact, do not uniformly affect the nature of the work of radio. An analysis of professional practice within the digital age reveals a great deal of variance in the range of activities, approaches and experiences with respect to time and techne, but a clear demonstration that the affordances of the digital environment are incredibly significant across the board. For the radio professional, what constitutes 'work' is in very large part shaped by the media environment in which that work happens – and that in turn alters the daily life and temporal experience of that radio professional.

Localism and the Illusion of Localism

Computerised networking systems and other digital era technologies have in many ways contributed to (or at least allowed for) a centralisation and urbanisation of radio production and distribution. Other forces, such as legislation – itself a technology of control in the Foucauldian sense (Foucault and Kritzman, 1988) – or deregulation, the desire for greater profitability and increased labour efficiencies, the contemporary political economies of radio broadcasting, changes in ownership and priorities, and ever more sophisticated radio scheduling software, have each played their part in this shift in the institutional form of radio.

My own experience of radio centralisation came as production manger at Radio Pacific in New Zealand in the early 1990s. The radio station was already networked around the country during certain parts of the day, but it had local programming at other times. A Radio Pacific station in Invercargill might, for instance, carry the national overnight programme directly from Auckland but have its own local programme in the middle of the day – or at least one originating closer to home, say, at Christchurch, which is at least on the correct land mass. One of the key reasons for having this regional breakout was the fact that, together with regional sales representatives, the Christchurch broadcast team was able to play local commercials alongside those of national clients during its local programmes. Auckland or Wellington-specific advertisements seemed of little relevance to South Island listeners and provided a reason to turn off – besides, with local frequencies being able to sell airtime to local businesses, the advertising revenue offset the cost of locally sourced programming.

Managing Director Derek Lowe was keen to leverage technology to facilitate a style of networking that allowed for the sale of commercial airtime to multiple regions across the country, while making further cost savings by seamlessly incorporating those separate regional commercial schedules into a single nationwide programme. To that end, Radio Pacific was a testing site for software engineer Matthew Reid's early installation of the Airwaves radio scheduling and billing software. The software's capacity for audio digitisation and playback and the ability to remotely trigger regional commercial playback were first trialled in the Radio Pacific installation.

With the introduction of Airwaves software (later an RCS product), radio stations had access to a more flexible, multi-station system that not only digitalised accounts receivable and commercial scheduling, but seamlessly integrated it with billing, contract confirmation, management reporting and audio playback. Reid's Airwaves system was specifically designed to be incorporated with digital recording and playback of commercials on radio. At Radio Pacific commercials started to be added to the increasingly digital production pathway, and these were both produced in the Auckland studio and incorporated into one single nationwide programme. By 1993 Radio Pacific had five defined regions around the country with their own separate commercial schedules that were inserted into the single, uniform, networked programme. Computers in each region were updated using Bernoulli discs dispatched by overnight courier from the Auckland head office and managed by a skeleton staff at each remote location. The disks, though cumbersome, could contain up to 90 MB of uncompressed audio data files in a package resilient enough to survive an overnight courier to the regions where it was uploaded and integrated into the on-air schedule – before being returned for erasure and the addition of the next batch of localised commercials, station promotions and their playback schedules. All of the commercial schedules were created at the station's head office, and all of the network's commercials were produced in the two studios located in Ponsonby, Auckland. The production flow bottleneck was severe, so any opportunity to streamline production processes was a practical matter of urgency.

The effect of this kind of networking was to give a sense of relevance to local listeners – to create an illusion of localness. While the programme content itself became focused on the national rather than the regional, the specificities of local interests gave way to a more generic and national perspective on current affairs, all of which emanated from the country's largest, most populous and most urbanised metropolitan area. While callers to the programme came from around the country, this shift to a national focus with regional commercial breakouts was a significant effect of the affordances of the new technologies – as were the inevitable job losses, staff relocations and redundancies.

These processes of centralisation and attendant loss of regionalism, localism and representation of the specific characteristics of smaller communities have been a common feature in the broadcast radio industries in both music and talk formats in New Zealand and around the world. As a result, the representations of daily life in different places formerly given a voice and reflected in local radio have, over time, been effectively eroded in many ways. This is not to say that there aren't counter-examples; and digital technologies have also facilitated the rise of some forms of hyperlocal radio, including micro-broadcasting and online-only stations that focus on a particular community. But at the macro-level the forces of deregulation, centralisation and aggregated ownership, as well as the ability to broadcast targeted commercial content simultaneously, in the context of a nationally syndicated radio programme, have been widespread and dominant.

Representing Daily Life

Radio's relationship with 'daily life' goes beyond the simple experience of radio as part of everyday activity, whether as a consumer or as a producer of programming. Daily life – or at least its representation – is also very often the content of radio texts. In fact one could make a case that radio's real text, rather than being 'the clock on the studio wall' (Garner 1990: 194), is a catalogue of human life, thought and expression.

National Public Radio's *This American Life* is a programme that purports to deal with exactly this topic: stories from the everyday, as well as from the unusual parts of life in the United States. The unique and often groundbreaking approach to narrative that this programme has adopted will be explored in greater detail in chapter 5. For now, my interest is in the reflection of what actually constitutes daily life and how it is experienced. Topics covered by *This American Life* that relate directly to digital technologies are quite diverse: computer hacking (in a programme on the nature of sin); computers that can detect smell (in a programme about mapping the world); computer dating (in a programme about authenticity); the pervasive nature of digital communications (in a programme about invisible worlds); online video technology as memorial (in a programme about birthdays, anniversaries and milestones); computerised voting systems (in a programme about the gap between theory and practice); and the ways in which we connect and speak to each other in the online environment (in a programme about the ways in which how we communicate has changed over time). In one episode, *This American Life* dedicated a full hour to the conditions of daily life in an Apple factory in China (Daisey 2012), which was later the subject of some controversy. This is explained on the 'This American Life' website:

> NOTE: This American Life has retracted this story because we learned that many of Mike Daisey's experiences in China were fabricated.

Other than highlighting the possible sensationalising of the working conditions of factory employees as a part of the representation of daily life in the digital age, this short explanation also yields another couple of interesting observations. The first regards the extent to which public radio has an air of authority about the way the world is. Bob Garfield's opinion piece in the *Guardian* expresses a betrayal that in many ways recalls what must have been felt by those who fell victim to the sheer believability of broadcast programming evidenced in Orson Welles' famous *War of the Worlds* dramatic broadcast, which fooled many of its listeners:

> I had more than once uttered the words, 'How could a performance artist have so scooped the whole world of journalism?'
> Here's how: by making stuff up. By reporting the presence of non-existent child laborers. By cutting a poison-chemical incident that occurred in one Chinese factory city and pasting it into another. By crafting a narrative not from the significantly impressive facts but from the glittery geegaws of the plausible. (Garfield 2012)

But perhaps even more telling than the sheer authority of public radio broadcasting evidenced in this instance is the fact that the story itself – one of outsourced factory workers experiencing atrocious conditions at the hands of the world's biggest corporation (significantly, itself a digital technologies company) in an era of corporate, globalised capitalism – appeared to be so immediately persuasive and convincing as to not require external verification prior to broadcast.

Meanwhile, the mediation and representation of daily life itself, as told through news and sport broadcasts, magazine-style programming such as Radio New Zealand National's Kim Hill Radio Show, journalistic non-fiction such as *This American Life*, and BBC radio drama series such as *The Archers* all have become profoundly different in an era of digital technologies. Language, concepts, activities, ideas and the stuff of everyday life in general have changed within the digital media environment to the point where to talk (or sing) about concepts like the internet, Facebook, downloading, text messaging, copyright infringement using digital technologies, the production of music on laptop computers, Skype calls, digital photography, YouTube and much more has simply become part of everyday discourse – as routine, mundane and part of one's lived experience on radio as anywhere else.

CHAPTER FOUR

The Sound of Music

Radio is inextricably linked with music, and especially with recordings of music. For decades a synergistic relationship between the radio industry and the record industry has existed in which radio provides the recorded music business with perhaps its best promotional tool, while the record industry in turn provides radio with a never-ending supply of popular programming content, not simply in terms of records, but also in terms of artist interviews and other ancillary content. Over the years, largely through the medium of radio, music has provided a soundtrack to epochal cultural and societal change, and this has been highlighted and celebrated in films such as *American Graffiti*, *Good Morning Vietnam* and *Pump Up the Volume*. But, while both socially and culturally significant in terms of impact, the relationship between the two sectors (and indeed the very basis of that relationship) is a commercial one, inscribed by the logic of market capital and corporate cultures. There are, of course, musicians who just want their songs to reach the widest possible audience; DJs who want to introduce the music they're passionate about to their fans; and record companies who want to facilitate that process. But the context within which that happens is entirely constrained by commercial and other factors. As a result, that set of relationships has always been a contested and often a very tense one.

The development of digital techne has provided the ground for those tensions to be further tested and for that relationship to be even more challenged, at least in terms of the ways in which these synergies function. Both industries find themselves in more or less the same boat when it comes to the struggle with a changed media environment; each stakes a claim on the obligations the other has to its own interests, and yet both parties, while inextricably woven together in many ways, find themselves in a period of history where that synergistic hybrid can be renegotiated – and not purely on economic grounds (although, perhaps inescapably, to economic ends).

The institution of radio has long had a cultural and social role as a tastemaker and opinion leader within music scenes and subgenres. In the digital age, the medium appears to have some unique opportunities and advantages when it comes to addressing and responding to music fandom; this is done through a range of interventions that include diversified programming, technological and procedural innovation within existing radio station practice, the use of the internet as a source of market intelligence and understanding of fan practices and shifting tastes, and the development of online and other digital offerings to cater to increasingly fragmented niche and specialist music audiences. Of course, the opportunity to diversify, or indeed to appeal directly to music fans at all, is not on the agenda for many radio companies. Many prefer to use music as a way of constructing audiences through a reassuring familiarity rather than through an engagement with active fandom. And while there is a fairly clear relationship between radio airplay and commercial success for many recording artists and opportunities for radio stations to use that influence to their competitive advantage, it would appear that that powerful relationship strengthens rather than challenges the status quo. Berland's explanation of the seemingly 'natural' place of music within the radio media environment is useful:

> The assumption that music is the ideal programme content for radio rests on the equally convenient assumption that radio listeners are mainly not listening very closely and that this is the 'natural' condition for radio communication. Thus the flow of music offered by radio has become inseparable from the mental image of wallpaper which shadows the concept of 'secondary medium'. (Berland 1990: 180)

This notion of secondariness is echoed by Simon Frith, who notes the pragmatism behind the tendency to broadcast music that is familiar and unchallenging:

> [P]eople are more likely to stay tuned to a radio station the more likely it is to play music that is familiar to them, records that they already own or have just bought. It is much harder to maintain listening figures for programs or stations that routinely play the odd or unfamiliar. (Frith 1998: 97)

That said, while it is true that many large-scale traditional radio broadcasters still want simply to play the 'hits' and that major labels are still very keen to release records that achieve that status, there is an increasingly 'long tail' (Anderson 2006) of both radio and radio-like outlets and sources of what professional and amateur radio workers consider to be 'broadcast-worthy' music. What is interesting from the perspective of an observer of the media environment is the extent to which niche programming is becoming an increasingly mainstream activity, increasingly engaged with by large commercial and public radio brands as well as on community, college and low-power FM radio stations – not to mention the incredibly long tail of internet radio stations, streams, music podcasts and other radio-like services. This long tail of music and of radio offers a potentially radical diversification of that entire media ecology. There are significant examples of that potential being explored, and we will examine some case studies below. And yet, despite the seemingly 'democratising' affordances of the digital media environment, the phenomenon of safe programming and music radio familiarity does not appear to have changed significantly in the digital age, as the *Guardian*'s Helienne Lindvall observes:

> Yet, as research shows that radio is the chief factor in driving record sales in the UK – and that most record buyers only buy music on the iTunes front-page top 10 – some artists and their managers are now telling labels to revert to the old ways . . . (Lindvall 2011)

Once again, however, the music radio ecology is incredibly diverse and far from uniform in nature. While certain trends may appear to be obvious and significant at a macro-level, it is in the margins that the profound changes in any environmental shift tend to become evident. With that in mind, it is important to note that the examples of change within music radio in the digital age cited below do not constitute a body of evidence for a set of hard and fast rules or effects that now apply, nor for a set of essentialist, technologically deterministic events that are 'happening to' either the music or the radio industries – but rather for a set of affordances and effectivities that are being taken advantage of in different ways, negotiated and worked through in praxis. The complexities of these environmental changes within music radio are being constantly negotiated over time. My purpose is not to show you 'the profound thing that happened', but rather to draw attention to the significance of the fact that all of these things – and more – are happening.

There Is Already Music on the Radio

It is beyond the scope of this book to retell the history of the relationship between the medium of radio and the medium of recorded music. Issues and historical events – including the shift from broadcasting live performances of orchestras to the playing of records; the adoption of 'needle time' rules in the UK and elsewhere; the apocryphal story of Todd Storz inventing the Top 40 format for radio; and the 'good vs evil' discourse of late 1960s pirate radio battles both to champion popular music forms on behalf of a deprived public and to fight for the legitimation of private radio broadcasting – have all been endlessly and comprehensively rehearsed in a myriad of other books on the development of radio.

Let us start instead with the observation that a large proportion of contemporary radio forms contain music as a key part of their programming output; that the music included is chosen deliberately by somebody to perform a certain function; that this music has both a commercial and a political dimension to it and its use produces value for music creators and for music businesses as well as for the radio station and its audience; that the judgement of what music is selected to be played is subject to criteria that are strategic and commercial rather than merely aesthetic; that the playing (or not playing) of certain pieces of music both constructs audiences and reinforces power relationships between radio and record industries, while it also impacts profoundly upon popular culture; that radio remediates music and gives it a different set of meanings, contexts and uses; that radio broadcasting affects and changes the sonic properties of a recording; that listening to music on radio is an experientially different cultural practice of consumption from listening to music in other 'mediated' forms; that in fact, as Wall (2003: 108) points out, radio broadcasts of records are one of the ways in which meanings of popular music are created; and that certain conventions concerning the ways in which that music is arranged into a particular order and is deployed in different day parts in different ways have formed over time for technical, professional, discursive, political, economic, social and cultural reasons. These facts all appear to be broadly uncontroversial, but it is worth at least stating them before we can move on to discuss how these complex and contested factors fare within a changed media context.

The relationship between radio and music is already incredibly complex. And, likewise, the different sets of relationships that exist between the institutional forms of radio industries and music industries are similarly complex. I use 'industries' in the plural in both instances, because the range of different music and radio industries and their relationships to each other are each important. Beyond the obvious songs that get playlisted, presented and distributed as part of the text of music radio broadcasting, different aspects and manifestations of radio organisations interact with different types of music businesses for different purposes. Radio station promotion teams may work with live music event sponsorship; advertising copywriters and producers may include royalty-free library music within radio commercials; spoken word programme producers will deploy musical elements within radio dramas, features and documentaries; on-air presenters may choose instrumental music beds to play behind their spoken content; programme directors and station managers may commission jingles and musical station imaging . . . and so on. We may, in a study of music on radio, notice or pay particular attention to the frequency of occurrence of certain songs played throughout the day on a contemporary hit radio station, but there is far more to music on radio than the playlist and its rotate system. It's a crucially important element within music radio broadcasting, of course, but that specific use of music is not necessarily as important to radio as music's more general role within a broader framework that combines a range of different musical elements with other elements (speech and sound effects) to communicate, persuade, entertain and construct an audience, usually for commercial ends. A shift to a digital media environment necessarily therefore has a range of different effects and opens up a range of different possibilities within that complex ecology.

The reason that recordings of music and performances by live musicians appear on radio goes beyond the simple observation that radio is primarily an auditory medium. It might seem an obvious element to include within such a medium, but it is neither a necessary nor inevitable component of radio broadcasting. There are, of course, plenty of instances of radio stations that do not use music as the core of their programming – though I would suggest almost no radio stations that do not use music at all – but from its earliest days, the affordances of the medium and its technological environment and the hard-fought-for systems of control that both permit and dictate the terms of its inclusion, have led us to a point where music has, to a casual observer, come to seem a natural component and easy fit within what may be heard on radio.

Debates about whether the playing of recordings of the international repertoire is harmful to local, working musicians, or whether there should be a higher or lower fee (or any fee at all) paid to rightsholders and performers is one that has been addressed at length elsewhere (Ahlkvist 2001, Hendy 2000, Percival 2011, Sweeting 2006), as has the fact that the vast majority of music mediated by radio is produced by large corporations that are 'the main advocates, sponsors and beneficiaries of a thuggish, anti-democratic economic ideology responsible for shaping much of our social and cultural lives' (Fairchild 2012). While these are critically important issues, which will be addressed to some extent below, my primary focus is on the extent to which the relationship between music makers, music companies, music radio stations and listeners has changed in the context of the digital environment. In the previous chapter I discussed radio's relationship with the experience of time and the use of radio content by audience members in a digital environment, especially with respect to the opportunities presented by timeshifting. I suggested that 'interestingness' may be favoured over Berland's secondary medium characteristic of 'aural wallpaper'. The aural wallpaper approach to music radio broadcasting does seem to have dominated for a considerable period of time – though, of course, it was neither essential nor total, either in its adoption or in its reception. Even so, the idea that timeshifting may provide the impetus for a greater priority being given to music playlists and programmes with characteristics that would reward focused, deliberate listening (and that this might be considered a 'more natural' state for music radio) is certainly an interesting provocation for the digital age.

Radio as a Music Business

Although I have been deliberate in doing so up to this point, to speak of the radio industry as a separate entity from (and often at odds with) the music industry is in fact to misunderstand or perhaps misrepresent both. While there is usually a clear separation between the institutional form of the record company and that of the radio station, it is also important to make a distinction between the institutions known as radio stations and the radio industry, just as it is important to make those same distinctions between the institutions known as record companies and the music industry. In addition, as we have already seen, the age of digital techne has muddied the boundaries to the extent that a radio station potentially involves a good deal more (or, conversely, a good deal less) than simply the ownership of AM or FM transmitters and studios, employing presenters, copywriters, producers and technicians, having the lease of a broadcast frequency and licence, and broadcasting terrestrially within a geographically defined area in a linear, time-bound fashion. In fact this was not always entirely the case, and there are certainly many instances of radio stations prior to the digital age that break one or more of these conventions. Likewise, the music industries have always been diverse, multivarious and complex in form, and they are today increasingly so. Wikström (2009) divides the industrialised music businesses into three main components: the recorded music industry, the live music industry and the music publishing industry, a cluster in which the record business is currently (macro-economically speaking) only the second, or perhaps even the third most significant component (see Page 2010). But the three-part industrial-scale view of the music industries misses a lot of useful commercial activity and provides an incomplete picture of what that industry contains and entails. To that list of music businesses that make up the music industry, one could add music education, musical instrument manufacture and retail, music therapy, jingle and library music production, music promotion, music journalism, music television, music photography, online music platforms, music metadata, wedding DJs, music archives, and a whole range of other areas in which people make music the basis for commercial activity.

Wikström's division of the music industry into those three primary and commercially dominant components is not incorrect, as the latter describe an industrial domain at its macro-level.

But here I am interested in the (media) environmental shift that impacts upon an entire ecosystem of music-related industriousness, much of which happens at the micro-level and a good deal of which falls beneath the radar of economic indicators such as the readily countable index of those music businesses that are registered for VAT in the UK.

Just as other music media forms are part of the music industry ecosystem (for example music journalism, music photography, music television, music websites and online services), music radio takes its place within the promotional culture and is part of the promotional infrastructure of music industries virtually across the board, and not just at the macro-level. Artists are interviewed on air, songs are played and discussed by disk jockeys, concerts are promoted, music prizes are given away, record companies take out advertising for new releases, and so on. But, perhaps more significantly, rather than simply provide a marketing outlet for concerts and records, radio airplay also directly generates revenue on behalf of the record industry and for the composers. As with many such things, this fact is neither universal nor a natural right, but rather a series of complex discursive practices that are performed and debated between powerful interests in different contexts (usually at the level of the nation state). In these circumstances, it's worth pointing out that the kinds of agreements that have been settled upon in Europe and many other national contexts for these kinds of payments are not the same as those that have been negotiated in the United States of America, where performance royalties are not paid for AM/FM broadcast radio airplay. This is an ongoing area of dispute and is, at the time of writing, still being fought between radio and record company interests in US courts. In line with fairly globally accepted intellectual property remuneration practices, composers are paid for their works being broadcast, but there currently exists no performance royalty for American broadcast radio, even though it does exist for streaming services. Within that context, Recording Industry Association of America (RIAA) Chairman and CEO Cary Sherman observes:

> The bottom line is that every platform that legally plays music pays to do so – except for one. AM/FM radio stations use music to draw billions of dollars in advertising revenue for themselves, but they don't pay a cent to artists, musicians and sound recording owners who make the music they use. (CMU 2012)

The counter-argument put by the radio stations in response is that to pay those royalties would not benefit the artists in question, since the money is dispersed to the record companies and not to the performers (and certainly the track record of labels paying artists is historically poor); besides, having to pay those additional fees would cause job losses within the broadcast industry and would make many of the smaller radio stations commercially non-viable. They also argue that playing the songs on the radio pays the artists by promoting their record, as they get money from the sale of recordings. The point here is not that one side is right or wrong, but that this is a contested and complex commercial matter, with a range of different interests at stake, each party lobbying for what it perceives to be best for itself. And the broader point is that these movements of money do not take place between different or competing industries, but between different parts of what is ostensibly the same area of commercial practice: radio stations and record companies, which, much like each other, use the same creative cultural works as the basis for commercial exploitation within the same media environment. What is being debated is not whether the practices should take place, or whether the different industries are engaged in activities that are unfairly at odds, but simply how the money should be divided up between them. The relationships that exist between record companies and radio stations are closer than might at first appear – and, as Fairchild (2012) points out, these relationships are predominantly corporate in nature, often profoundly anti-democratic and, arguably, frequently corrupt. All the same, their general relationship is a synergistic one in the ecological sense that both organisms are inseparably entwined and their existence depends to a very large measure on that of the other. They are therefore, in these terms, part of the same industry, woven together and working in different ways with the same set of commercial assets towards mutual, individual and, at times, mutually exploitative goals.

But, apart from the complex and intractable relationship between radio and music organisations, Tim Wall (2003) makes a point about the role of music radio as music business that does not simply depend on a series of exchanges and expectations between professional organisations: he calls attention to the fact that radio's synergies with music do not lie exclusively with the latter's industries, but, more importantly, with its consumption cultures.

In 'a social critique of radio music' (1945), Theodore Adorno makes a similar observation: that the playing of music over the airwaves contributes to increasing standardisation and reinforces the commodity character of music. In other words, he argues that the music that radio plays affects the kinds of music that get made. The music radio industrial complex does not merely affect consumption cultures and the distribution of cultural artefacts and experiences, but also – and necessarily – cultures of composition and production. Further, argues Adorno, the soporific nature of music that is purely for 'entertainment' (a word he employs with some disdain) serves the purpose, intended or otherwise, of keeping listeners from criticising social realities. But, most importantly, Adorno recognises that there is a substantive difference between 'music' and 'music on radio'. McLuhan would later put forward the idea that 'the medium is the message' (1964: 7), but Adorno anticipates this observation by at least crediting the fact that there is a difference between them, and that the difference is significant. That is to say, while McLuhan would argue that by far the greater social and cultural force being exerted (particularly upon audience members) is that of the medium of radio rather than that of its content (in this instance, recordings of music), Adorno would note that it is the nature and meanings of music that are changed through the processes of broadcasting, and it is these changes that have societal effects. As Wall observes, just as a record is itself a fan artefact with its own connotations and significances for the music listener beyond the sound of the recording coming out of the speaker when it plays, radio is likewise a medium through which the meanings of popular music are created – and not simply the neutral vessel that conveys that recording, unchanged, from producer to consumer. Listening to music on the radio is in itself an important and specific set of experiences, meanings and interpretations, something that goes beyond simply 'listening to music'; and it feeds back into, and informs, the kinds of popular music that get made. And while this set of music consumption practices alters profoundly in the digital age, the fact that the fundamental relationship between audiences and the means through which they hear the music is important does not. When asked 'what are you listening to?', a listener might be as likely to say Wally Walker on KQRS as he or she is to say Elton John's 'The Bitch Is Back' (despite the fact that it may be the song that is coming out of the speakers, and not the voice of the presenter); as likely to say Spotify as the new Coldplay album; as likely (if not more so) to say the Metalheadz podcast as the Grooverider Remix of Goldie's 'Kemistry'.

So it is useful to consider music radio as part of the music industries, or at least as part of the musical industrial ecosystem – that single, inseparable set of relationships that construct, perform, distribute, consume, exploit, make meaning from and constitute popular music culture.

Generally speaking, when a biological ecosystem changes under the pressure of environmental forces, the smaller and more adaptable organisms that had performed peripheral functions in the earlier incarnation of that environment often take on a much more significant role within the new context, while large and specialist organisms tend to recede, in a shifting of ratios. This phenomenon repeats itself fairly consistently across a wide range of different ecosystems under conditions of change. Likewise (to extend the metaphor still further) the synergies that existed in a previous biological ecosystem are redrafted and renegotiated within the new environmental context. There may be new forms of organism in the mix, and some forms of organism may have changed in terms of their dominance (and in some rare instances may have entirely died out). This certainly appears to be the case with the shift in music industries in the changing digital context. Within this particular process of renegotiation, the consideration of music radio as a music industry itself and as an 'organism' that belongs in the music industrial ecosystem (that is, as a business that uses music as a means by which economic activity is generated and from which value is extracted) is a useful one. Therefore it is equally useful to examine the manner in which that commercial value is extracted from popular music. In the case of commercial radio, the value of music is in its power to assist in the construction and maintenance of an audience, which can then be aggregated and sold, usually in 30-second units of attention, to advertisers. In simple terms, music is not the product of music radio and listeners are not the target customers. Advertisers are the customers. The audience is the product. Music is, effectively, as Berland points out, the bait.

> Music-programming is not the main commodity produced by radio, but is rather the means to the production of radio's real commodity – the audience – to be sold to advertisers in exchange for revenue to the broadcaster. (Berland 1990: 183)

The primary purpose of commercial music radio broadcasting is thus to deliver an audience to a group of advertisers and sponsors. To achieve commercial success, that audience must be as large as possible. More than any other characteristics (such as demographic or psychographic profile, purchasing power, level of interest, degree of satisfaction, quality of attention or emotional state), the sheer quantity of an audience aggregated as a mass is the most significant metric for broadcasters seeking to make music radio for profitable ends. As a result, broadcasters attempt to maximise their audience size by playing music that is popular, or – at the very least – music that can be relied upon not to cause audiences to switch off their radio or change the station. Audience retention is a key value (if not the key value) for many music programmers and for radio station management. In consequence, as noted above, a high degree of risk aversion frequently marks out the 'successful' radio music programmer. Playlists are restricted, and often very small. The most popular music radio stations have entire catalogues of fewer than three hundred tunes and A-Rotate categories consisting of ten songs or less. In order for a song to make it into active A-Rotate, it will typically need to usurp the position of another song in that group. As a result, it is very difficult for record companies to 'break' new artists in the world of commercial radio, and even more difficult for new subgenres, for more exploratory works, and certainly for artists who fall outside of the London / New York / Los Angeles axis of popular, major label Anglo-American music prevalent on CHR stations the world over to assert themselves.

But to characterise all radio music programming simply as the choice to play whatever is safest to play is not only unfair, but also inaccurate – and in my own listening I have found more exceptions than examples that may confirm that hypothesis. While the 'safe' approach to music radio programming may be prevalent in many large, corporate-owned music radio stations across Europe, in the United States, Australia and New Zealand and so on, contemporary music radio programming in its broadest sense is incredibly diverse. In fact, a decade ago, even within American commercial music radio, Ahlkvist (2001) was able to identify four different music programming paradigms that he characterises as being based on the interests of aesthetics, audience, research and industry. While Ahlkvist did not identify the stations he visited or the music programmers he interviewed (which would have been incredibly illuminating in terms of matching espoused programming philosophy with actual station output), it is probably fair to say that most stations around the world find a balance in their music output between those four modes – or, perhaps more accurately, 'orientations'. To play a mix of songs that expresses a sense of what 'good music' might be (aesthetics); to put oneself in the shoes of the station's audience and hear the music through the perspective of uses, gratifications and emotional effect (audience); to base pro-gramming decisions on quantifiable indicators of 'what works' (research); and to support and act as a conduit for record compa-nies (industry) are not mutually exclusive propositions but rather a series of frequently competing interests that shape the context within which a music programmer or team makes a decision as to which records to add, play more often, or remove from the playlist. A music programmer may, for instance, express an audience orientation to his or her programming decision-making process, but this does not necessarily mean that the other factors are not also important considerations. That said, the digital environment provides an opportunity for music radio workers to reconsider and reimagine the extent to which those different aspects should have an influence over playlist deci-sions, playlist size, the inflexibility of the playlist and so on, from a purely pragmatic perspective that understands and reflects the changing nature of the environment within which that music is played. Specific music, played in an order on the radio, creates meaning for audiences. But the way in which that meaning is constructed and the context within which that meaning is made have changed.

Niche Audiences and the Construction of Musical Taste

One of the key roles in music radio has been its part in the cura-tion, formation and negotiation of public tastes when it comes to popular music. And, despite the preponderance of familiarity, conformity, 'secondariness' and conservatism among music radio programmers, which was noted by the likes of Frith and Berland above, there is also a strong sense in which music radio does not merely reflect public taste and comfort its audience with what it already knows and likes, but it may also play the role of a gatekeeper determining popular taste (Rothenbuhler and McCourt 1992: 101). As always, the truth is more complex than either of those positions might suggest, and radio neither leads nor reflects taste exclusively. However, those seemingly mutually contradictory activities engaged in by music radio highlight the complexity of the relationship between the cultural phenomenon of taste formation and the jointly persuasive powers of the recorded music industry's marketing efforts and music programmers' skills in building playlists that couch the new among the familiar in order to contextualise, give meaning and make connections for audiences. So to look at music radio as either leading the music consumer by the nose or simply pandering to the simplicity of the audience's unchallenged and unchallenging collective tastes overlooks the very significant roles that radio stations, radio shows and radio presenters often have in the complex negotiation of taste. Indeed some radio programmes become iconic due to their reputation for consistently introducing music fans to new music and artists, in a format that helps to construct a sphere of shared cultural tastes outside of the mainstream. A case in point is university-based Santa Monica public radio station KCRW's *Morning Becomes Eclectic*, which, despite its espoused eclecticism, provides an international focal point for discerning indie rock and folk music fans, and it does so through its online stream and on-demand listening possibilities. This programme occupies an influential position within specialist music taste beyond the boundaries of its own FM coverage area, and it has been instrumental to the development of the careers of artists such as Sufjan Stevens, Mumford and Sons, Beck, Adele and many others. *Morning Becomes Eclectic* is not only influential among fans of independent music; it is also closely followed by record label A&R personnel. The programme itself has been on air for over 30 years (since 1978), though its global influence has been furthered through its online activities. KCRW archives and makes available for download its in-studio performances as podcasts, and it streams its programmes in a number of different formats, which can be heard by using software such as iTunes. The position of radio presenter as tastemaker is significant within the context of the radio programme itself, but it has ramifications across other media forms – for instance, hosts of *Morning Becomes Eclectic* have gone on to choose music for film and television. The contribution of KCRW's presenters to contemporary popular taste (particularly with respect to independent pop music and its fan cultures) has been estimable.

In addition to flagship programmes that introduce listeners to new artists within established popular music traditions, some broadcasters will make use of the niche and subcultural fan activities and enthusiasms of the presenters themselves through specialist programmes and variations on playlists; and in that context an influential individual with a platform can have a good deal of impact in the shaping of entirely new music scenes and subgenres through the medium of radio.

A good recent (digital age) example of this phenomenon is British DJ and radio presenter Mary Anne Hobbs, whose programmes formed a focal point for the development of new electronic music forms, perhaps most notably that of dubstep. Hobbs profiled artists and recordings that were not distributed through the mainstream channels of the popular music industries, but instead represented and championed alternative music cultures and independent music businesses, collectives and hobbyist activities conducted within initially very small subcultural groups. Of course, Hobbs' programme was not the only media outlet paying attention to these musical forms and, significantly, online radio stations and pirate FM stations sprang up from within those same (and connected) subcultures to champion that music as well. However, as a broadcaster on popular music station BBC Radio 1 for 14 years, Hobbs was in a position to reach an audience that might not otherwise have had access to or knowledge about that musical subculture. From playing in underground clubs to initially very small audiences in London, artists such as Skream, Benga, Kode9, Burial, Rusko and Caspa came to find both a regular and supportive nationwide outlet and, subsequently, an audience for their music that ultimately contributed to the position of dubstep as a popular cultural force; and this may not have been possible without that degree of exposure and curation. There are several important things to note here, of course. First, that dubstep did not arrive fully formed and did not remain unchanged throughout that process of popularisation. Second, that the weekly radio broadcast was not the sole causative ingredient to that electronic music subgenre's rise to its current cultural significance. And, third, that the people listening to the music were not simply its consumers; in many instances they were themselves producers (or future producers) of dubstep and other alternative electronic music forms.

The digital media ecology within which Hobbs' late night Radio 1 show *The Breezeblock* (later, *Experimental*) was broadcast was significant. People did not simply listen to the radio programme and then go to clubs or buy records. Instead the show formed part of a complex ecosystem of electronic and digital media platforms. Artists and fans distributed the music in ad-hoc networks of filesharing and CD burning; they recorded unauthorised mixes and transferred tracks between mobile devices via Bluetooth. Producers shared their music online (more recently on Soundcloud and YouTube), not just as a way of providing an opportunity to hear the recordings outside of a club or radio environment, but also a way to build discussion around the music and to create a community of fans familiar with a canon of popular and influential tracks within the scene. Scene-specific subcultural fan practices began to be formed and propagated. The comments on dubstep releases, particularly on YouTube but also on Soundcloud and elsewhere, developed their own patterns of discourse around how 'filthy' the sounds in the song were (often with competitively obscene and scatalogical references, made for humorous effect), how heavy the 'drop', and so on. In addition, discussion groups such as Dubstep Forum feature a range of message boards in which fans discuss the music, the club nights and other matters, as well as share mixtapes and off-air recordings of radio programmes such as those on Rinse FM and Hobbs' own show. Significantly, many producers of this and related electronic music styles (including some key innovators in the scene) use Dubstep Forum to give newcomers feedback and technical advice for working with different music production software in order to develop collectively an aesthetics and a broad scope of competencies and skills. In this way a series of conversational and mixed-mode digital media platforms that relate to and include the radio broadcasts have enabled the scene and its sounds to become widespread in music consumption and production subcultures. Within this broader context of discursive practice, Hobbs' flagship Radio 1 show provided a focal point for consumption, discussion, fan practice and tastemaking that helped to define an entire musical scene, which has gone on to have a significant influence on the sounds and palette of popular music almost right across the board.

That Hobbs' show did broadcast late at night on the BBC is significant. Radio 1's role as a public broadcaster with a remit to carry specialist music forms – rather than as a commercial radio station with an overriding responsibility to its shareholders – means that risks can be taken and that the enthusiasms of individual programme makers and presenters can be indulged to a certain extent. This is not to say that public broadcasters are free of the pressure to maintain or grow audience sizes or that programmes are free of the pressure to prove their value for money, but rather that the opportunity existed to make use of the BBC's policy towards specialist music. In our article on specialist music fans online, Tim Wall and I discuss that policy as follows:

> For the BBC specialist music is 'music which appeals to specific groups of listeners – focusing on a specific genre of music or on cutting-edge music from a range of genres'. This definition places an emphasis on the ordering of music by its listeners as definable groups, and the link of these social groups to genre-specific music, or a notion of the music as innovative. Implicit in this definition is a distinction between a majority mainstream, and a series of minority 'taste groups'. This is, of course, made explicit in the BBC's practice which reproduces this distinction within its broadcast schedule as daytime = wide appeal; evening = specialist (= small audiences). So fundamental is this calculus to public service broadcasting as it relates to music radio, that it has been articulated in the statement 'ratings by day; reputation by night' (Wall and Dubber 2009: 28).

In the electric age, the choice to broadcast niche musical styles or to introduce new music to listeners has been, for station programmers, a difficult trade-off, a 'zero-sum game' risk and a commercial decision with potentially severe ramifications, due to the limited availability of on-air time and to the scarcity of the broadcast spectrum. However, one of the affordances of the new media environment is to challenge the notion and the nature of that scarcity.

There are radio organisations that have recently chosen to address niche interests and tastes, while making use of the ability to broadcast more in a day than can fit into 24 hours in 'real time' on air: they do this by using streaming media and web content to add supplementary material, and even extra radio 'channels' dedicated to subgenres and related fields of music. For example, French station Jazz Radio broadcasts a single programme nationwide on 39 frequencies across the country. It also has 23 different 'web radio' streams that cover everything from Latin jazz on one channel to 'Christmas jazz' on another.

In the United States, satellite radio provides another opportunity for a greater diversity of music programming across a wide range of channels. Garth Alper explains:

> Out of the over 120 channels currently broadcast by XM, 67 of them are devoted to music. Each music channel is commercial free and broadcasts 24 hours a day, seven days a week. All but a few of these 67 channels are devoted to a single genre or sub-genre of music, which contrasts sharply with the approximately ten to 15 music formats commonly heard on present-day commercial radio. The remaining few XM channels air mostly eclectic programming aimed at a particular age group or demographic. (Alper 2006: 507)

Thus the opportunity for the specialist music fan to find something that is more suited to a specific taste, or for the curious music listener to select a broader diversity of styles, discover new artists or learn more about different musical subcultures is certainly made possible through this implementation of digital technologies. However, that affordance is at odds with a range of competing factors and is subject to other environmental forces, not least forces of an economic nature. In a private correspondence six years after that article was written, Alper explained to me the effect of the merger of the two competing satellite radio companies (Sirius Radio and XM) in terms of musical diversity:

> Several channels outside of the more mainstream pop, rock, jazz, classical, country, and hip-hop genres were victims of the XM/Sirius merger that took place in 2008. Some examples of channels that were terminated: 'Beyond Jazz': progressive jazz; 'Aguila', regional Mexican; 'The Rhyme', early hip-hop; 'Fuego', reggae and Hispanic; and Ngoma: African music. Before the merger, XM and Sirius were touted for programming a diverse lineup of lesser-heard genres and sub-genres of music, but the discontinuation of these and other channels was injurious to one of satellite radio's strengths. (Alper 2012)

There are presently (according to XM/Sirius' own genre classification) only three jazz channels on Sirius: Real Jazz, which covers the mainstream jazz movements of the past 70 years; Watercolors, a smooth jazz format; and Seriously Sinatra, which broadcasts the singers of 'the great American songbook'. Arguably, there is scope for some greater segmentation of jazz programming, while at the same time, by over-segmenting, perhaps unnecessarily, other musical genres (there are 24 rock channels, for instance), Sirius gives the appearance of providing greater choice, but significantly reduces eclecticism and serendipitous discovery within each individual channel. For this reason, satellite radio in the USA is an interesting case in the competing interests, effects, opportunities and constraints of music broadcasting in the digital age.

High Fidelity

Alongside increased choice, one of the key marketing features of digital radio platforms such as satellite radio in the United States or DAB in the UK has been the audio quality of the programme

output. An early description of DAB radio in *New Scientist* magazine paints the picture thus:

> Imagine driving the length of Britain, over the Channel and
> across Europe, listening all the time to the same radio station.
> The sound is in digital stereo, which gives it the same quality as
> that from a compact disc. There is no interference and none of
> the fading and fluttering that normally blemish reception as you
> drive past tall buildings, over hills and down valleys. (Fox 1991,
> quoted in O'Neill 2009: 270)

While neither the trouble-free and ubiquitous reception nor the
trans-European coverage of a single radio station have come to
pass, the promise of CD-quality audio hasn't either – and significantly so. Technically speaking, CD-quality audio consists of
uncompressed digital data sampled in 16-bit quality at 44.1 kHz.
That said, through digital compression techniques, it is possible
to make substantial (and important) bandwidth savings by reducing the amount of information used to capture and communicate
that audio without significantly reducing the perceived audio
quality of the broadcast. MP3 files work in this way – discarding
data elements that (at least theoretically) do not noticeably alter
the overall sound of the music. These 'lossy' files may not be
acceptable to the most discerning of audiophiles, but in a listening context such as a kitchen benchtop radio or a car stereo the
impact of light-touch data compression is typically not so great
as to make one quibble about the veracity of CD-quality claims.
From a technical perspective, nobody realistically expected DAB
radio to actually transmit music in a lossless format, though
music fans who looked forward to a marked fidelity improvement over FM broadcasting were in for a disappointment.

DAB radio stations are not each allocated to an individual
broadcast frequency in the way AM/FM broadcasts are; instead,
a particular frequency block carries a multiplex that can be
coded to carry between 5 and 10 individual radio signals (Lax
et al. 2008). The bandwidth of the entire multiplex is fixed,
and so, in order to increase the number of channels per multiplex, reductions in available bandwidth for each station are

necessary. In the UK the number of stations that can be put on a particular multiplex is not mandated through regulation but subject to the strategic commercial interests of the multiplex leaseholder:

> the Authority is not empowered to specify the types or numbers of digital sound programme or additional services which it expects to be provided on a multiplex. (Radio Authority 2001, quoted in Lax et al. 2008: 161)

As a result, competing potential affordances of the DAB framework (that is, the opportunity to extend listener choice and the commercial opportunity to profit from the maximum number of radio signals within a multiplex) tend to overrule the affordance of increased audio fidelity. In fact music enthusiasts often complain that the data compression used in order to fit more 'radio' onto the radio means that the sound of DAB broadcasts is now inferior to that of analogue FM broadcasts.

This is not to say that CD-quality audio is not possible with digital radio formats (not even that it represents a theoretical upper limit), but simply that, to date, audio fidelity has not been an affordance of the media environment that has been taken advantage of by radio institutions, and indeed by radio-like music services. There is a trade-off between the cost of providing high-fidelity audio on the one hand and the other affordances and limitations of the various digital media forms of radio on the other; hence, to date, audio fidelity has not been a priority. While there is little immediate opportunity for radical change in the delivery platform of DAB or satellite radio for instance, for reasons of widespread adoption of reception equipment, infrastructural investment and the like, in the broader digital environment the cost of increased bandwidth and processing has reduced remarkably, while capacity and speeds have increased. It is conceivable that digital radio platforms based on traditional terrestrial broadcast models will eventually fall out of favour with broadcasters and audiences alike as the capacity of internet bandwidth increases, broadband coverage reaches saturation, mobile data becomes increasingly inexpensive, and so on. In that instance, a potential shift to radio over internet protocol (IP) becomes not just a technical possibility, but also an opportunity for further development in the area of audio fidelity – and this for the simple reason that bandwidth limitations do not apply in the same way as they currently do with existing DAB technologies. To be clear: they do apply – just not in the same way. As Stephen Lax points out, with the current technologies and at current bandwidth costs, streaming high-fidelity radio programmes to large audiences is prohibitive – though there are opportunities for strategic uses of its capacity to address the problem of audio-quality shortfall on existing digital radio services, where the need is felt to be greatest:

> For example, the BBC transmits its classical music station, 'Radio 3', on FM, on DAB, and it also streams in so-called high definition sound via the Internet to satisfy those who wish to hear classical music at higher audio quality. These audiophiles, the 'golden ears' as the audio engineers describe them, who typically will link their computers to a hi-fi system to benefit fully from the audio quality, are fortunately relatively few in number, and so can be served by the BBC's data streams. (Lax 2011: 157)

While ever greater audio fidelity may be a desirable outcome for radio's music fans, radio's potential as a communication and entertainment medium in situations where bandwidth is a challenge could be argued to be one of its strengths. But, without wishing to make predictions about an uncertain future subject to a broad range of variables, it is possible to imagine that, under conditions of increased capacity, cheaper data streams, more widespread and more reliable high-speed mobile data transmission, greater uptake of devices capable of receiving large quantities of data at low cost (especially without being tethered to cables and telephone lines), consumer demand could conceivably increase for this sort of service and the number of so-called 'golden ears' may turn out to be greater than the BBC audio engineers whom Lax describes might have imagined. What's more, they may not all be classical music fans.

Replacing Music Radio

In addition to the process in which previously existing music radio stations have been shifted to digital formats and the introduction of new (though traditionally formatted and presented) music radio stations on digital platforms, there are now several online music services that not only emulate some aspects of radio, but deliberately use the discourse of radio to explain and promote what they offer. Online music services, such as Pandora, Last.fm, Spotify, Rdio and Deezer each use the language of radio broadcasting as metaphors for their own offerings. It is certainly fair to suggest that these services, in different ways, address many of the uses and gratifications usually attributed to music radio. In short, it is possible to listen to streams and playlists of music that one does not necessarily own the recordings of, and these may be presented in such a way as to construct a coherent musical narrative or set of cultural meanings; for instance, a channel based around a particular song or artist may be internally consistent and agreeable to a listener in a manner that resembles a specialist music programme or favourite radio station. There are, of course, obvious differences between what is traditionally thought of as radio and these automated, on-demand, generative and individually tailored music services. In fact, other than the observation that, when you turn it on, music comes out, the similiarities with music radio broadcasting can appear rather slim.

But, as I have been careful to stress throughout this book, the concept of what is or isn't radio is less interesting than the discursive categories through which we might discuss the features of these media forms with their often overlapping technological, cultural, social, infrastructural and environmental characteristics. In other words, a discussion of whether Last.fm is or isn't radio is not a useful debate to have, simply because answering that question fundamentally rests upon being able to establish an essentialist definition of radio. That is, in order to be radio, something must have a certain set of non-negotiable characteristics. I happen not to think of any of these streaming services as being 'radio', but the fact that this is how I think is, on the one hand, a function of my age, set of experiences and personal interpretations of different media; and on the other, entirely immaterial in terms of an analysis of radio in the digital age. The fact is that all of these services self-identify either as radio or as having radio content as part of their fundamental makeup. As a piece of discourse, we must initially take this at face value and, instead of arguing whether the Spotify Radio service really is radio in any meaningful sense, we should seek to understand the phenomenon of Spotify Radio within the media ecology it comes from and in the context of the affordances and effectivities it utilises.

But to think of these services as simply being like radio on the internet (a phenomenon that actually exists separately, in a number of different ways) does them a disservice and fails to acknowledge the advantages they have taken of the affordances of the digital environment, which provide for them their distinctive and innovative break with music media forms of the past. Some of these services break away from the centralised model of broadcasting by using peer connections and networks. Others use rich and deep databases to construct individualised playlists based on the comparison of metadata. For instance, the way in which Last.fm's radio service makes meaning from music is a social way. That is: 'people who like the artist whom you like also like these other artists'. Your friends, with whom you have compatible taste to different degrees, share these musical interests with you – and so here are some other things that you may have in common. So in that respect your music stream is based on a social graph of musical connections. In contrast, Pandora, while still experientially a music stream based on your initial parameters of taste, makes meaning from music musicologically. That is, the song that you like is of a particular musical genre, key and tempo, and has been coded with certain characteristics such as a male or a female vocal, instrumentation and other characteristics of the arrangements, and so on. So Pandora will play you other music that shares those musicological characteristics. That it serves a function as an individualised, tailored musical experience is what it shares with some other online music services, but the architecture, method of delivery and means by which it makes meaning from music are worthy of investigation on their own merits. Whether or not it's useful to make decisions about whether it 'counts' as radio seem an irrelevance in that respect. As a method of categorisation, the word begins to lose its usefulness with respect to these services. The fact that a discourse of radio is built around these services for promotional and conceptual reasons – even if only metaphorically – is interesting because of what this says about our cultural baggage and understandings of the discursive meanings of radio: that radio is something you listen to; that its primary code can be music; that it has a role in taste curation and music discovery – and so on.

Perhaps the most important aspect of these online music services is the audience perception that the music comes from 'out there' somewhere and that, by making connections between music recordings, meaning is being made. Songs are meaningful in and of themselves, but there is a further musical and deeper cultural meaning that may be derived from them in this order. In that respect, Pandora, Last.fm, Spotify and other online streaming music services that use the word 'radio' to describe an aspect of their offering – without any of the institutions, devices, production technologies, professional practices, or transmission architectures of previous, electric age incarnations of radio – perform a music role that is homologous to that of radio. And while one might idealise the notion of a human curator with advanced specialist knowledge choosing what to play and constructing the programme with an understanding of how one song follows another, how segues are constructed and what meanings different songs can have in ways other than musicological or social – these automated, personalised services at the very least start to address the perennial hope of the serious music fan radio listener: that they might play something that I like next . . .

CHAPTER FIVE

Stories in the Air

It's a useful cliché, repeated by practitioners and radio educators alike, that radio is 'theatre of the mind'. By telling stories using words, music and sound effects, radio can engage the imagination to communicate ideas and images that create a kind of narrative uniquely experienced by each individual listener. Through the omission of visual cues and by embracing the openness of the work (Eco 1989), radio storytelling has the capacity to make personal connections, paint pictures with sound, and indeed create scenes that would be impossible in another context. The capacity of audio as a medium for imaginative and compelling storytelling is undiminished in the digital age, although the production, distribution and consumption cultures and technologies through which those stories are mediated have radically changed. In fact the possibilities for radiophonic narrative are in many ways expanded in the digital age, as research engineers, professionals and enthusiasts explore the parameters of new production processes, platforms and interactive opportunities, as well as opportunities for radio storytelling to be taken outside the realm of the radio professional.

Some things remain constant in the digital age, however. The tale of how the dramatisation of H. G. Wells' *War of the Worlds* presented by Orson Welles in his series 'Mercury Theatre on the Air' convinced audiences of an alien invasion and caused mass panic is well known; but the fact that contemporary audiences are more knowing in this respect does not stop false information or fantastical stories from being believed and acted upon today.

At the same time developments in technology, availability of digital sound libraries and access to sophisticated production

processes on affordable equipment have all allowed even amateur radio storytellers to aspire to more ambitious sonic aesthetic
goals, to be achieved for instance by adopting naturalistic, cinematic or otherwise innovative approaches to the use of sound
in support of that 'theatre of the mind' process. Digital technology has enabled radio storytellers to take listeners on an
imaginative journey in ways never possible before. However,
alongside the 'emancipatory' narrative possibilities facilitated
by digital technologies, an increasing number of pressures
just not to tell stories any longer have also arisen. The automation, digitalisation, and ever tighter radio formatting that have
enabled radio institutions to make efficiencies in production
and in human resources have left little room for experimenta-
tion and deviation from what is considered to be more 'regular'
programming. As a result, documentaries, drama, and those
imagination-based radio programmes that fall between the gaps,
while scarce to begin with, are even harder to find on the
airwaves.

Additionally, story-based children's programming appears to
be less common on radio across the board as televisual, interactive and game-based screen media increasingly claim the role it
once occupied. Budgets for radio drama and documentary storytelling are being almost uniformly cut, and drama departments,
where they exist, are constantly being asked to do more with
less – and, often, less with less. While opportunities open up for
digital producers to make innovative and previously impossible
or impractical narrative forms, the mechanisms by which the
craft skills of dramatic production are traditionally passed among
radio producers are designed out of the system, and so many
young producers are left to reinvent the wheel. And, as news stories unfold in a world of the internet, social media and 24-hour
rolling news coverage on digital television channels, radio may
have lost its edge of immediacy. But at the centre of both music
and speech programming is narrative form. By construction,
almost any radio programme takes the shape of a story – at the
very least, in the Aristotelian sense of having a beginning, a

middle and an end. There may not be conflict and resolution, characters may not learn and grow and narrative archetypes may not be referenced, but the momentum and shape of narrative as a sequence of events that build and grow upon each other permeates radio broadcasting, online and off. And there is a simple reason for this: radio, like all media forms, is simply a means by which human beings communicate with each other. As Mark Turner asserts, narrative mechanisms are cognitive structures deeply hard-wired into the human mind. '*Story* is a basic principle of mind. Most of our experience, our knowledge, and our thinking is organized as stories' (Turner, 1998: v). We tell each other stories. That's what we do. Radio is one of the means by which we do that.

Narrative and Production

The ability of the spoken word to communicate ideas and understanding is at the heart of human communication. The propensity to take those words and fashion them into stories is central to that process. In the *Cambridge Introduction to Narrative*, H. Porter Abbott goes further, to suggest that this capacity for storytelling is both innate and fundamental to what it is to be human:

> Given the presence of narrative in almost all human discourse, there is little wonder that there are theorists who place it next to language itself as the distinctive human trait . . . Whether or not such assertions stand up under scrutiny, it is still the case that we engage in narrative so often and with such unconscious ease that the gift for it would seem to be everyone's birthright. (Abbott 2008: 1)

Given this innate and dominant nature of storytelling with respect to the ways in which we take in and make sense of information about the world and our relationship to it, the changes to the media environment I describe in the opening chapter of this book also affect the nature of the form of the very ingredient that is at the basis of who we are. In other words, as the form and structure of narrative changes, so do the ways in which we are human beings.

Radio storytelling, in its various forms, appears to differ in character from place to place. This should not surprise us, as the conventions of different national and local radio narrative styles are necessarily shaped by the personalities living there, by the geographically specific political economy, local colloquialisms, dialect and storytelling traditions of the place, and by the specific tropes of radio that are established, repeated and developed over time within any localised broadcast radius. There is no one type of radio storytelling any more than there is only one type of folkloric tradition or accent. There are, of course, and there have been for a long time, globalised instances of radio content. Internationally syndicated radio programmes such as Casey Kasem's *American Top 40* and its predecessors provided a template for the much repeated narrative convention of the countdown show, with its various rises and falls in chart position and the big revelation of the 'number one' song in the country providing the dénouement – at least for that particular week.

Likewise, there appears to be a universality in the way in which radio news is delivered: the voice has a particular cadence regardless of the language used, and the structure of big national stories, big international stories, local stories, human interest stories, sports news, then weather and traffic provides a rough template for almost every bulletin on every station the world over. The mix of global and local traditions, conventions and tropes gives the world of broadcasting a range of different radio narrative styles, which are at once identifiable as radio storytelling but also as, say, British radio drama (specifically, Radio 4 drama) and the panel show format; US public radio current affairs storytelling (such as the programme segments in *All Things Considered*); New Zealand student radio advertising; Australian radio art; Canadian documentary; and so on – in ways that go beyond being able to identify the speakers' accents. That is not to say that a piece of radio is essentially British, American or what have you – but perhaps rather typically.

As a result, conventions of format and production approach (as well as of speech delivery) differ from place to place. However, with increasingly globalised access to media forms, these conventions, which have developed over time, may now be more readily adopted and brought into other spheres. Radio producers have the opportunity to learn not only craft skills but also philosophical and creative approaches to the medium from their international peers, and far more readily than ever before. The art and craft of telling stories through the medium of human voice, music and sound effect has the potential of yielding a broader and richer palette, as a result of the affordances of digital technologies of production, consumption, and – importantly – conversation.

Radio with Pictures

Perhaps the single most challenging and confrontational aspect of the digital age for the world of radio is the growing pre-dominance of screen-centric digital media platforms. Radio can be listened to on laptop, desktop and tablet computers, on digital television sets and on mobile phones. Even devices sold as radio receivers (such as DAB radios and car stereo systems) are increasingly likely to have a screen-based interface and the affordances of displaying and conveying visual information in a way that has previously been outside the realm of traditional radio broadcasting. RDS (radio data service) text information conveys small amounts of digital information within the ana-logue FM broadcast, allowing radio receivers to display the name of the station, the song being played, the name of the show – and even to give instructions to the radio receiver to change channels or switch off a CD player at a particular moment – a process to be initiated at the broadcaster's end – so as to make room for impor-tant news or traffic information. The level of interactivity, at least in terms of metaphorically allowing the broadcaster to reach into your car and change the channel for you, makes for quite a profound change in terms of the way in which the experience of radio listening is shaped in the digital environment and of the powerful affordances that this offers consumer electronics manufacturers as well as broadcasters and listeners. Putting a text screen on a radio is not a trivial alteration to the media context, but the beginning of a profoundly altered relationship between broadcast institution and private listener.

Of course, as technology develops and the platforms on which radio storytelling can take place proliferate, the opportunities that screen media present to the world of radio keep expanding. Benjamin Chesterton is a UK-based former BBC radio producer who turned to audio slideshows as a way of storytelling using digital multimedia. His company, duckrabbit, was founded on the principles of using radio production techniques enhanced with visual imagery in order to convey the same kinds of stories that one might tell on the radio. The still images in these 'photofilms' support the audio rather than dominate the experience of the storytelling and lend themselves well to portable media platforms such as mobile phones. They provide an immersive listening experience, with a 'glanceable' visual element to them. To the extent that they represent a radiophonic way of telling the story, they retain audio's affordance of being consumable while you are engaged in other activities – such as walking and watching where you are going – but they also make use of the fact that the device on which you are consuming this audio content also has a screen. The visual imagery adds depth and a secondary sense impression of the material.

One excellent example of this is a story created by duckrabbit trainees Ciara Leeming and Oliver Edwards, entitled 'Zen and the Art of Sandcastles': it is a story reflecting on personal loss that is told through the spoken word recollections of a professional sandcastle builder, and it is interspersed with audio of a man helping a group of children build and then destroy their own sandcastle. The audio carries the story, though the visuals add richness, poignancy and depth to the piece, and also convey deeper information about the context and character of the people whose voices appear. Using the affordance of the digital medium

– not simply making television or video instead of radio but adapting radio techniques to the digital medium – allows for new types of stories to be told in new ways: in this instance, visually enhanced radio storytelling. And while the editing process and final output of these 'photofilms' owe a great deal to video work, the audio-led approach to the construction gives the storytelling a strong radiophonic flavour.

Of course, it doesn't necessarily take a radio producer to marry still photography with audio elements, nor is it necessary for the audio to lead the storytelling. An iPhone application called Picle captures sound when photographs are taken, and these photographs-with-sound can be ordered, stitched together into a slide show and exported to YouTube. From there, the photofilms can be shared across social networks. While typically these multimedia productions are impressionistic (in the sense that the app captures the ambient sound while the photo is being taken) rather than constructed as a traditional story, it is possible, with some consideration, to build a story through speech, actuality and photography using the app. Developer Alex Harding of Made by Many, in his introductory video to the application, describes the relationship of images to sound with respect to a visit he made to the beachfront town of Broadstairs in the south-east of England: 'We could go there any day of the week and capture the same pictures. The sounds that belong with that picture are unique and of that moment' (Harding 2012). In other words, the primacy of the audio in capturing and retelling the story of a particular moment in time is, to Harding, the key strength of the addition of sound to pictures (or vice versa). A still image is exactly that: still; a moment frozen. It is impossible to freeze sound in time, as sound is a durational experience. That is, stopped sound is silence. Hence to capture a brief duration of audio is to place the still image that goes with it in the context of motion, of progression and of narrative momentum. Moreover, by utilising the affordances of available technology both to capture images and to record audio, to marry those two together and to offer the users the possibility to construct from a series of picles, one creates a product in which a narrative of the user's choosing can be shared and told. As a result, the mobile phone is deployed as a production device as well as merely a consumption tool.

Another example of a marriage of audio storytelling with pictures, and also with text, is the website Cowbird, which offers a range of tools for people to tell their own stories online. The site aims to 'build a public library of human experience' and, while it does not appear to mention the word 'radio' as part of the language used to talk about the site's methodology and philosophies, many of the stories featured on the site have a clear connection with the traditions of radio storytelling (although not every vignette is audio-based). A picture and either descriptive text or a transcript of the spoken word content accompanies each of the stories, which are frequently personal and, again, impressionistic. In fact it would seem that the affordances of digital techne made use of within the Cowbird community encourage certain types of storytelling (and even a particular aesthetics) over others. For instance, while it would be technically feasible for Cowbird to allow video submissions or to develop a mobile app with which users could submit stories, the website's designers have chosen not to take advantage of those technologies, in order to prioritise a particular kind of engagement. Like in many radio programmes that feature a range of different contributors, the context shapes the overall feel of the 'programme'. And, while Cowbird does not really resemble a radio programme in any other way, the storytelling ecology it facilitates shares certain characteristics with this kind of context. That is, when you 'tune in' to Cowbird, your expectations of a certain kind of storytelling are typically met, albeit with a broad diversity of voices and subjects being represented and even though the community is made up of members of the public with no particular training or specialist instruction. The aesthetics and the conventions are shaped by the architecture of the site and arise from the community itself. The narratives explored within Cowbird and the technologies it deploys may not necessarily have unique antecedents within the radio medium, but there are clear radiophonic qualities to many of the stories; in much the same way, the audio slideshows of duckrabbit utilise radio techniques and evoke radio storytelling in a context that would appear to be, in the most meaningful respects, entirely outside of the medium of radio.

Marrying pictures with radio storytelling has perhaps been most ambitiously attempted by the National Public Radio show *This American Life*. The programme tells stories using a range of different narrative techniques; but it has developed, over its years on air, a unique and identifiable approach, pace and production aesthetics. The show has been turned into a television programme by Showtime, which endeavoured to retain that same aesthetics through the use of tripod-mounted cameras rather than creating documentary-style actuality captured through the use of handheld cameras, and by applying a cinematic approach to the visuals. The result was a television programme that emulated the feel of the radio programme through its use of the human voice and of incidental music as the drivers of plot and tone respectively; and, interestingly, while moving images were used throughout, the pictures that enhanced and supported the storytelling tended to be framed as still images and shot more as photographs than as video. More recently, the radio programme simultaneously ventured into cinema, theatre, the web and a range of other media forms, both online and off, through its live show *The Invisible Made Visible* (Glass and Chicago Public Media 2011). The radio show was recorded and performed in front of a live theatre audience and filmed for live simultaneous distribution in cinemas around the US, Canada and in Australia. In recognition of the affordances of the stage and screen, the two-hour show was designed in such a way that a full hour of the performance was so visually based as to be entirely unrepresentable within the context of an audio-only radio programme. However, the remaining material was designed with the listener in mind, so that there would be enough content for the full weekly on-air radio show as well. The contrast between the different parts of the material (from simple spoken word to acrobatics and mime) demonstrates the parameters and possibilities of the different media forms – and very consciously and deliberately so. And – while the live performance used computer-generated graphics and featured a high degree of interactivity through the use of a mobile application that allowed audiences to play along with a performance by the band OK Go (not to mention the fact that the video of the live show is available to stream or download from the radio show's website, as is the one-hour radio programme) – perhaps the most interesting affordance of the digital technologies being utilised in this scenario is the ability to transmit to, and to involve, live audiences in cinemas across the globe simultaneously. While the ability to transmit television pictures worldwide without the aid of internet technologies has been there for long, the capacity for high-speed data transfer of the high-resolution images that are needed to fill a cinema-sized screen is something that developing digital technologies, fibre optic connections and powerful digital video and audio processing have all made possible. It is worth underlining, of course, that this is not a regular feature of the *This American Life* radio programme; nor is it likely ever to become one, or so it seems. It is instead an instance of a traditional radio show experimenting with the form, limitations and content of radio storytelling through the use of other media forms, which have become available for exploration through the use of the radio programme's format, character, key ingredients and programme shape (if not its duration and strict character). *This American Life* is a show that looks to reach as wide an audience as possible in as many different ways as possible – through archiving, podcasts, modularisation, streaming, on-demand listening, downloadable transcripts, the television series, and this live, recorded, online-distributed, interactive and purchasable media product, which bears the same brand as well as the hallmarks of 'radio-ness' that the programme is known for.

Another approach to the marriage of visuals and radio broad-casting is what is often described as 'visualised radio'. An example of this is Radio 1's *Official Chart* show, which marries live video footage of the radio presenter with music videos, which are synchronised with the songs played out on the radio broadcast. The programme goes to air live and follows all of the narrative conventions of the music countdown shows described above, but differs from most music radio shows in that it is possible to watch the show live online, as it is being broadcast. There have long been examples, of course, of radio studios that have webcams in them, and it is possible to see what presenters are up to while they go about their work. However, in this instance, the BBC brought some television techne to bear upon the programme. By cutting between several different camera angles within the radio broadcast studio itself, host Reggie Yates is seen to perform his work as the programme's presenter, and, when he plays a song, the music video replaces the image of him in the studio.

My own listening and research for this book happened to coincide with the broadcast of the first instance of this multimedia broadcast experiment by the BBC, and there were some interesting observations to be made at the time about the uniqueness of that first broadcast, not least that the interest created among the programme's listeners, coupled with the high-bandwidth requirements of video content, brought the Radio 1 website to a standstill. Perhaps the most interesting aspect of that particular evening's chart show, however, was that the Nicki Minaj song 'Starship', which was number 7 in the charts that week, did not appear to have an official promotional video to accompany it, and so in the week leading up to the broadcast the BBC Radio 1 official Twitter account had been used to ask listeners to submit videos of themselves dancing to the song. Minaj retweeted the request to her nine million or so followers, and Radio 1 was very quickly able to edit together fan-generated content into a music clip that went out on the website while the *Official Chart* show was being simulcast.

Radio as Social Object

The widespread availability of digital editing tools allows for people to engage with radio content in new ways, which have the potential to convert passive listening into modes of speaking. By capturing, excerpting and remixing pieces of radio and online audio content, listeners are able to incorporate radio content into their own online conversations. In this manner, just as digital videos, songs and photographs have become included into online sociality, audio content can become part of the ways in which people construct and engage in conversation. This is to say that the digital audio media files become shared 'social objects'. In my article about a practice-based online music research project I conducted in India, I explain the theory of social objects in the following way:

> In a conversational medium, where the communication is predominantly many-to-many (as opposed to broadcasting's one-to-many mode), the sharing of social objects becomes a primary activity through which engagement takes place. And it is 'sharing' that is key to understanding this kind of media engagement. Audiences (if that is the appropriate term) do not merely consume online media, but repackage, recontextualise and reinterpret. (Dubber 2012: 22)

The idea of social objects (at least in a media and cultural studies tradition) is traceable to Jaiku founder Jyri Engeström (2005) and follows from the work of Knorr-Cetina (2001), who emphasises the differentiation between subject and object in activity-based knowledge acquisition. On his blog and in his public presentations, Engeström has applied the core of this idea to the practice of engaging in relational online networks such as Facebook, Twitter or fan message boards. This concept of object-centred sociality online was later developed through a series of blog posts by cartoonist Hugh MacLeod (2007); but, fundamentally for both writers, the notion of social objects provides a frame through which social engagement online can be understood, and in particular strategised. Moreover, shared objects are central to the ways in which people socialise, both online and off. That is, they do not simply talk – they talk about something. It is Engeström's contention, for example, that social networks that simply try to connect people without a specific object or objective engage merely in the meaningless collection of contacts and connections ('friends'), and their emptiness and lack of genuine social activity around some sort of focal point or object of interaction inevitably spells failure. Taking further the centrality of the social object as an item around which conversation takes place, MacLeod (2007) interrogates the notion of social object in terms of the way in which it creates meaning. To MacLeod, the object is social in the sense that its very meaning is socially negotiated. Objects are shared in order to provide the occasion for conversation, though they may not necessarily shape or relate to the content of that conversation. In other words, the social object might not be what the discussants are talking about online, but it is the reason why those particular people are talking. As McLeod suggests, 'the interesting thing about the Social Object is not the object itself, but the conversations that happen around them' (ibid.).

According to Yrjö Engeström (2000), the ways in which learning and knowledge are generated and shared and from which meaning is derived take place with respect to an object, and within an environment that has other actors as well as norms and regulations. The object-oriented activity is therefore also, and importantly, a social activity, and one that is in part directed and inscribed by the context within which that activity takes place. For instance, computer-mediated communication (and remediation) is shaped by the affordances of the technological medium of the computer.

An example of this phenomenon is explored in Sam Coley's (2012a) examination of fan practices with respect to a documentary about David Bowie that he made for New Zealand public radio. As a veteran popular recording artist, Bowie has a substantial and active worldwide fan base, with a strong interest in media content about the object of the shared fan activity. As such, the documentary *Bowie's Waiata*, which contained a never heard before recording of an original Bowie composition, became the subject of much online discussion. As Coley explains:

> [O]n 24 November, 1983, Bowie was invited by the indigenous
> Maori tribe 'Ngati Toa' to visit Takapuwahia marae in nearby
> Porirua. The invitation was a rare honour at the time and saw
> Bowie become the first rock star to be officially welcomed onto
> a Maori marae. Remarkably, Bowie composed and sang an
> original song for the people of Ngati Toa that was captured by a
> radio station that was also present. The song was never officially
> released and was only heard on the marae that day in 1983 and
> in a radio news report on Wellington's 2ZB the following morn-
> ing. (Coley 2012a: 83)

After 25 years in storage in a New Zealand radio station, the
song was unearthed and became the central focus of the radio
documentary programme and series of audio slideshows created by Coley to commemorate that event. The programme was
broadcast on Radio New Zealand National and simultaneously
streamed live online. It was also archived on the Radio New
Zealand website, so that audiences could listen on demand. Fans
were thus able to listen and discuss the programme, and, as a
Bowie fan himself, Coley engaged with the fan communities to
talk about the meanings in the programme, the cultural aspects
of the marae visit, the meaning of waiata, and so on. I interviewed Coley about his observations of the online fan reactions
around his documentary, and while he agreed with Engeström
and MacLeod about the way in which fans used the media
content to express and discuss their fandom, there were some
unexpected aspects to this matter. For instance, the Bowie fans
would not simply share links to the documentary, or even create
excerpts in order to start a conversation with others about the
material content of the programmes, but would instead rework
the material, re-editing it to create new content from the 'raw
material' of the radio broadcast. Coley ventured an opinion as to
why this might be the case:

> I think it's interesting with Bowie because he hasn't released
> anything new for a decade, so fans are cannibalising, in a sense,
> his past work and his past stories in order to satisfy their crav-
> ing for new Bowie content . . . so I think there is a desire to be

associated with the story of Bowie and to continue it with their own creativity and insights. (Coley 2012b)

There are, for instance, several versions on YouTube of the segment of the radio documentary that contains Bowie's previously unheard song, each accompanied by a slideshow of images. The 'official' version was made and uploaded by Coley himself, and it contains the original full-quality programme audio as well as some pictures of Coley with backing vocalist Frank Simms and with members of the Maori tribe who were present at the event; and there are also re-edited fan-made versions, which appear to use a recording of the low-quality online stream of the radio broadcast, and a slideshow of different photos, sourced from the internet. In this way fan discourse around media texts takes on a creative aspect. And, while it would not be true in any useful sense to describe these practices as 'interactivity' or 'collaboration', they are engagements with the text and patterns of discourse that are facilitated by the media environment within which the activities take place. That creative response to the object of fandom has antecedents, of course, in other media contexts (for instance in the creation of fanzines and newsletters); however, the speed, sophistication, reach and impact of the digital fan creations is noteworthy. If they do not represent a categorically different set of cultural practices, then they are certainly radically different in terms of their conversational nature and social purposes. Fans not only remade the content and reproduced it as an instance of fan art, but also interrogated the text, asked the radio producer himself for further information, discussed instances where clarity may have been lacking, pointed out where there were inconsistencies or inaccuracies, and provided alternative versions of that particular part of Bowie's narrative. In conversation, Coley related the fact that, while the attention of fellow fans was a positive thing for a producer of such a documentary to receive and while to be able to share such an exciting and previously inaccessible media text with them in a way that allowed them to express their enthusiasm was gratifying, from the point of view of the creator of a radio programme there are also practical and pragmatic uses of that fan discourse that can feed directly back into the professionalised radio production process:

> As a producer, having that feedback is not just about gratifica-tion, it's about continuing the story, tying up loose ends . . . if there is an error, it's nice that in the comments section that can be put straight perhaps – or another perspective offered. If someone questions the veracity of something said by an interviewee, it at least posits other interpretations. I'm actually making another version of that documentary for broadcast in 2013 – the 30th anniversary [of the album *Let's Dance* and the 'Serious Moonlight' tour that supported its release] so the feedback that I've got from fans has informed my future docu-mentary production . . . (Coley 2012b)

As Engeström and MacLeod explain, the online conversation around a social object need not necessarily be 'about' that object itself, and certainly does not go in a way that has been intended or imposed by its creator. The creator of the original media content can control neither the destiny of that content nor the context within which it will be discussed, reinterpreted and incorporated into the broader field of discourse. In that respect, the conver-sational online communication in the realm of fan producer/consumers differs fundamentally from that of broadcast media, in which the context, transmission and readings of the content can at least be reasonably predictable, if not responsive.

The implication of this is profound for creators of radio programming – and all the more profound from a cultural and societal perspective, given the sheer proliferation of radio and audio media producers, as well as the widespread de-profession-alisation of digital techne. Media makers can seed discussion and allow the discourse and the media production that ensue to inform and contribute to their own further practice; but they do not control the agenda. Creating what is now ultimately share-able and remixable media content is a process of creating social objects whose key value is 'interestingness', but which may be employed in different ways in order to support or provide context for any number of different discussions – as well as simply to supply raw material for other media products. In this way, with respect to media texts such as radio documentaries moving outside of a broadcast environment, the internet can be understood as a vernacular medium in which ideas and discussions are forming in, around, and through the use of social objects. Coley reflects upon that engagement within a vernacular medium, in relation to his own approach to the raw recorded material from which he constructs his radio storytelling production. One advantage, he claims, is that there is very little wastage:

> Whereas the decision to delete used to be a tough one for me, in this day and age, it's much simpler because I know that I can take any content that I wouldn't put in the transmission broadcast and leave it as an extra on Mixcloud or Soundcloud or something – a 'deleted scenes', if you will – which makes that editing process much easier because I don't have to struggle with 'I can't leave this out – it's too good'. I can always say to myself 'right, I'll put that in a separate category and give it to the audience to play with – see what they make of it'. (Coley 2012b)

Personal Radio Storytelling

One significant characteristic of the digital media environment is the increasingly accessible and affordable nature of media production tools that are available to non-professionals. Anybody with a smartphone, for instance, has at his or her disposal a media production tool rivalling in many ways (not least by being portable and easy to use) much of the expensive professional equipment available to radio producers just 20 years ago. This does not mean that everyone is now a radio producer, but rather that years of training, membership of a guild and employment status are no longer barriers to getting started in the world of media production. However, rather than creating a wave of amateur radio producers acting in competition with trained, professional broadcasters, the opportunities for radio storytelling opened up by this development can be utilised by radio stations and professional producers in order to make new types of programming, which encourage broadcastable submissions from listeners – user-generated content, in other words.

The BBC's Listening Project captures intimate conversations between non-professionals – 'regular' people talking to each other about things that are important to them. The project encourages people simply to record their conversations by using technologies that are readily available to hand and to submit these digital recordings for inclusion into a series of programmes that are then woven together, post-produced by BBC staff and broadcast across the BBC radio network. In addition, the recorded stories and interviews are archived by the British Library as part of a rapidly growing digital oral history of the United Kingdom. It is clear that the simplicity and widespread availability of the digital tools makes the capture, editing, photographic accompaniment and submission accessible to a far wider cross-section of the national population than has ever been possible, and the BBC project has made a point of reinforcing and supporting that process through the sharing of simple production knowledge, which is intended to give some basic media competencies and confidence to interested participants: 'Don't worry if you've never recorded anything before. We've written a simple step-by-step guide – all you need is a computer, laptop, camera or phone with a microphone' (BBC 2012).

The project is inspired by Storycorps, which 'aims to provide Americans of all backgrounds and beliefs with the opportunity to record, share, and preserve the stories of our lives' (see http://storycorps.org/). Storycorps goes a step further in facilitating the collection of stories by providing a specialised iPhone application, which allows users not only to listen to stories, but also to get tips and advice on how to record and interview. The app itself is also a very user-friendly piece of software with which to capture and submit the audio. In other words a small, virtually ubiquitous digital device contains within it the possibility, for almost anyone who may wish to do so, to consume radio stories and to learn how to create them, as well as the equipment with which to record and craft them, and the tool with which to submit them to a distribution platform and on to find an audience.

Audioboo is another mobile application and web platform for non-professionals – and professionals alike – to tell their stories, record and publish audio. The service adds a social element to the sharing of audio recordings, and as such it employs the strategic advantage of digital media as a social object. Like many other services that permit users to update their status, it facilitates the 'following' of interesting people, provides a stream of recent content, and also facilitates the sending of private direct messages to other users of the service, allowing for an internet-mediated voice messaging service. Some radio professionals (for example BBC technology journalist and commentator Rory Cellan-Jones) are regular Audioboo users, but the primary use of the site appears to be for personal reflection: audio blogging. The architecture of the application prioritises the capture and submission of audio with a sense of immediacy that makes highly produced, multitracked and professionally crafted studio creations far less common on the site than the simple sound of a person talking within an environment. As an addition to the ecology of radio-like storytelling platforms, Audioboo favours and facilitates a particular niche within its environment.

Learning to Make Radio Stories

The craft skills of radio storytelling are learned in different ways. My own trajectory from young, would-be sound engineer to producer of syndicated radio drama, documentary, music and entertainment programmes in the 1990s followed a trajectory of internship, on-the-job training, mentorship, watching over people's shoulders, studying works I admired, trial and error and, quite often, just getting it wrong in interesting ways that I then repeated and called 'my approach'. I have passed on some of these skills and philosophical approaches in a more structured manner within formal educational institutions over the past 15 years. However, the development of the web as a medium through which skills are transferred and through which learning takes on a far less formal and more conversational aspect means that, together with the proliferation of inexpensive production tools, other opportunities have arisen for amateurs and budding professionals simply to begin making stories and to have them heard and critiqued. Not only that, but – as Roman Mars, creator of the 99% Invisible podcast, discovered – it was also possible to make a living simply by creating and releasing stories. After producing his show for some time and distributing it to an audience that had grown to tens of thousands, he launched a Kickstarter campaign to raise money so that he could continue the programme on a professional basis: to make it his business rather than his hobby. He set a goal of $42,000. His audience gave him $170,000. As *This American Life* host Ira Glass observed in his 2012 Commencement Speech to the City University of New York's Graduate School of Journalism: 'One of the great things about [journalism today] is you don't have to wait for permission. You don't have to wait for somebody to give you a job to start making something that you think would be good' (see the video of his speech at http://vimeo.com/55563744).

Moreover, access to some of the world's most respected practitioners and teachers of radio storytelling has never been greater. An important site for the propagation and discussion of radio craft is Transom.org, which is billed as a 'showcase and workshop for new public radio'. Transom.org contains examples of radio storytelling and discussions of those works. It contains 'manifestos': long-form essays about the approach to radio writing and production authored by veterans of American public radio such as Jay Allison, the Kitchen Sisters and Ira Glass, who not only talk about what they consider to be the important elements of radio programme making, but also offer, within the body of the text, links to audio examples to support the points they are making. In addition, the website contains a wide range of resources, equipment reviews and collaborative online workshops in which works are created and peer-critiqued. In the 12 years (at the time of writing) that the website has existed, a wealth of knowledge and examples has been archived at Transom.org, and this constitutes an invaluable resource for students of radio storytelling, as well as a broader set of influences and provocations for existing radio practitioners. The site does have a distinctly (and unapologetically) American public radio focus, and its stated ambition is to foster and encourage more stories for that broadcast context; but radio enthusiasts worldwide use the site, and the eventual platform for the pieces that the site's users create need not, of course, be that context.

There is, however, a route to public radio broadcast in America for these kinds of stories that doesn't appear to exist in the same way in many other national public broadcasting contexts. Whereas in Britain the BBC's commissioning process is a formal procedure that requires the involvement of an approved independent radio production company and an array of forms to be filled in, public radio in the United States will often broadcast programmes submitted to the website Public Radio Exchange (PRX), which is an 'online marketplace for distribution, review, and licensing of public radio programming' (see http://prx.org). Members of the website can submit, review and discuss radio programmes that the website then makes available to public radio broadcasters through a licensing process that ensures that creators get paid for their submissions if these are aired. The content is sourced from independent and amateur producers around the world, but it is primarily broadcast on local public, community, college, and low-power FM (LPFM) stations in the United States. As a result of the political economy and history of American public radio, which bears very little resemblance to the form and structure of, say, British public radio, that broadcasting ecology lends itself more readily to this decentralised and localised programme commissioning and licensing methodology.

In the explanatory animated video on the website (PRX 2003), the Public Radio Exchange is described as being interested in everything, from 'veteran producers with a classic documentary to high school students with their first story', in order to create 'a Long Tail of public radio'. The democratic nature of public media is highlighted in the discourse around PRX, and the ability for the public to be heard rather than merely spoken to and to engage with critical issues through the medium of radio storytelling is cited as an emancipatory characteristic of the online environment – not as a platform to replace radio broadcasting, but as a means by which listeners and producers can connect with broadcasters in new ways, so that those stories may find an audience.

News Stories and Immediacy

One of the many areas in which the affordances of the digital technological environment have been taken advantage of so as to affect radio storytelling profoundly is in the realm of newsgathering and news production. Perhaps most obviously, the use of the smartphone as a small digital recording device has not only made the lot of the roving radio reporter less onerous in simple terms of sheer baggage, but has also made possible the editing and delivery of news stories via FTP, email and other electronic means. While a small smartphone touchscreen might not be the ideal interface for fine audio editing (though there are some very feature-rich audio editing apps available), it is certainly possible to trim and compile spoken word pieces for audio broadcast; and, while it falls outside of broadband wi-fi coverage, 3G internet is, generally speaking, fast and robust enough to manage the transfer of compressed audio files from the field.

But the affordances of smartphone technology go far beyond convenience and portability for professional news reporters. What has changed, again, is the degree to which professional and near-professional quality tools are in the hands of people outside the radio industry. Not only is anyone with a smartphone also thereby carrying a camera; he or she is also equipped with a small but powerful computer, a microphone and audio recording equipment, and the ability to record and post journalistic, editorial and documentary content. However, public submissions to professional radio broadcast news organisations often take the form of pictures and text rather than of audio recordings. Moreover, those pictures (and the associated written content for use) might not be submitted directly to the professional broadcasting organisation, but rather posted to public social network platforms. By following hashtags and by trending topics on platforms such as Twitter, professional journalists can have direct access to information in the field from citizen journalists and from observers who post online their reactions to events as they occur. The news organisation has the capacity to act as an aggregator, filter and fact checker for information being gathered around the world, and this simply through the act of people living their lives in public through digital social media and via mobile tools.

One example of this phenomenon from my own radio listening and online experience was the September 2010 earthquake in Canterbury, New Zealand. The 7.1 magnitude quake occurred at 4:35 a.m. local time, which was late afternoon for me in England. People from New Zealand whom I follow on Twitter immediately started reporting on the event as it appeared to them, and I tuned in to Radio New Zealand's live internet stream to hear information about the earthquake, seemingly before the Wellington-based station had started reporting that anything was going on. Because the event happened so early on a Saturday morning, both the media organisations and the official emergency response teams such as the police and the fire departments were operating on an overnight staff rather than with full media support and news teams. Radio New Zealand National's pre-recorded early morning children's storytelling was interrupted with 'unconfirmed' updates from the overnight on-air presenter. At first the children's stories were resumed, before the incongruity and discontinuity became too much, and the stories were replaced by filler music that would allow for regular interjections. As the day progressed and the information from official sources trickled in, Twitter was abuzz with people giving (and retweeting) eyewitness accounts of their personal experiences of the quake, its after-effects and the after-shocks.

Significantly, however, in a time of emergency, the public of New Zealand looked to the radio for authoritative information, as the radio broadcasters looked to social media and online communication tools to facilitate the building and telling of stories, soliciting and collecting personal reflection as the basis of news stories to supplement and give a greater depth of nuance to the official reports.

In other words, the flow of news and information happens in a variety of directions all at once, radio reporting finding itself in a new ecology, in which it still has an important role to play but where the voice of eyewitness needs no intermediary or official approval in order to be heard. This is not to say that radio becomes unnecessary or unimportant: radio proved to be an indispensable source of emergency and civil defence information as the day of the Canterbury earthquake progressed; but decentralised, digital, many-to-many media forms challenged the traditional perception of radio's primary position with respect to immediacy. Immediacy, it seems, is much swifter in the digital age.

CHAPTER SIX

Radio and Technology

The connection between radio and technology is central to almost any discussion of the medium. The discovery of the electromagnetic spectrum and the ability to transmit signals wirelessly were fundamental to the medium's invention, development and refinement in its early history, and the way in which that particular technology works provides the context for every discursive category up until (and to a large extent also well into) the digital age. In fact, phenomena that had constituted the technological truisms of radio prior to digitalisation contributed to essentialism and determinism in the analysis and explanation of radio, especially in discussions of audience effects, uses and gratifications. How radio always was, technologically speaking, was the frame through which how radio worked (and worked on us) was always viewed. Because radio had never been configured in any other way, it could not have been conceived of in any other way.

From the earliest wireless telegraphy to the transmission of voice and music over the airwaves to the contemporary commercialised and public service forms of radio broadcasting service, the machines and tools that enable and facilitate this form of media communication have been the framework on which what we call radio was built and around which all of our discursive categories revolve – from public policy to text, from professional practice to promotional culture. It seems an obvious thing to say, but, without radio technologies, there would be no radio. But it's important to underline this seemingly trivial observation, because, in a changed technological environment, it is precisely this ecosystem of technological forms that has changed

125

so profoundly. Even if we disregard the means of distribution, or even the kinds of programming that can get made, it should be a great surprise to us if radio as a media form had not significantly altered as a result of changes in the workings of those technologies it depends upon. The physical devices used in order to create, distribute and consume radio texts are, almost all, fundamentally different in the digital age, even when the primary method of transmission may, on the face of it, be identical. In other words, the way we make radio has changed even in those instances where the way we distribute it has not.

In the radio production studio, digitalisation has not been a simple process of switchover from one format to another. The shift from recorded tape to a complex combination of compact disc, DAT, MiniDisc, integrated digital audio workstation (DAW), editing software and studio-quality microphones with built-in digital recorders has been an ongoing process, and it is one that I observed unfold in my role as production manager at Radio Pacific in Auckland in the early 1990s as well as in my subsequent radio career elsewhere. While tape cartridge, vinyl and reel-to-reel technologies had remained largely unchanged for 40 years, the introduction of digital audio saw rapid change within studios as stations and managers endeavoured to keep up with rapid developments and swift obsolescence: from early experiments with pulse code modulator (PCM) 'black boxes' that would record digital audio onto the picture part of VHS tapes through to ADAT, the Orban Audicy DAW, ProTools, Soundscape, Sonic Solutions and CoolEdit Pro (later known as Adobe Audition). Likewise, innovations in advertising scheduling, billing, music programming, on-air playback and so on all underwent a process of rapid change and development over a very short period of time. There were competing platforms for each, leading to format incompatibilities between (and sometimes even within) radio stations. New digital technologies for use in radio stations had a tendency to be skeuomorphic (that is, they resembled earlier technologies in design and function), so digital audio editing on a screen resembled (it often still resembles to this day) the practice of splicing magnetic tape; music programming software emulates index cards in separate category boxes, arranged into packets and drawn on in order to create a playlist. At the heart of this skeuomorphism was the desire to minimise the learning curve for existing radio practitioners, so that the use of the new technologies would be intuitive and the transition from analogue techniques as smooth and swift as possible.

The Two Digitals

It is necessary here to underline my earlier distinction between two types of digital. In one sense, digital is the counterpart of analogue in terms of recording and distribution methodologies. In the other sense, as discussed in chapter 2, digital is the successor to electric in terms of a historicised media age. We use both analogue and digital technologies in the digital age, and the difference has to do with the extent to which the information is either continuous (analogue waves) or discrete (binary digits). The practice of analogue broadcasting on the AM and FM bands still exists, and the analogue nature of those broadcasts lies in the fact that they modulate waves within the electromagnetic spectrum. Analogue recording captures sound as waveforms (for instance, as continuous grooves on a vinyl record), whereas digital recording captures sound as a series of ones and zeros in a computer-mediated context. Analogue technologies were developed within, and are themselves characteristic of, the electric age of media. However, analogue forms of distribution and audio capture still persist in the digital age, although the way in which they are used, the kinds of technologies they connect with, and even the tools with which we deploy those technologies have themselves undergone significant changes.

The development of AM/FM reception equipment has progressed from the vacuum tubes and transistors of the electric age to the digital integrated circuit of the digital age. A single chip is capable of performing the complete radio tuner function, from antenna input to audio output, complete with automatically calibrated tuning and seek functions, processing and displaying the European Radio Data System (RDS) and the North American Radio Broadcast Data System (RBDS) with digital FM stereo processing, error detection and correction, and even clock functions. There are, on the market, several such chips available for electronics enthusiasts who may wish to build their own – very affordable – radio receivers, or devices that contain them. Likewise, these chips are mass-produced for devices such as mobile phones and bedside alarm clock radios, home stereos, car radios and portable listening devices. Such chips are integrated circuits belonging very much to the digital age, although their primary purpose is to receive and output an analogue transmission.

It is, of course, possible to make, transmit and receive analogue radio broadcasts without the intervention of any digital technologies whatsoever – it would just be very, very uncommon to do so in this day and age. The transmission technologies of AM and FM radio, while fundamentally analogue, exist within a very digital world – as, of course, do the production technologies that go towards making the programmes we hear on those analogue frequencies. In fact there is very little that remains analogue about AM/FM radio. The fact that it is broadcast over the electromagnetic spectrum as a series of waves is, of course, something that is, by definition, analogue – but of course many digital radio forms are also distributed via that same electromagnetic spectrum by using similar technologies, even though the information is encoded and decoded in a very different way at either end of that transmission. DAB radio in Europe, or satellite and HD Radio in the United States, all rely upon the electromagnetic spectrum to transmit their digital signals, just as AM and FM broadcasts do for their analogue ones. They may operate at different frequencies or be encoded and decoded using a different methodology, but, ontologically speaking, in the digital age both digital radio broadcasters and analogue broadcasters make radio texts using digital technologies and distribute them using analogue technologies; and these texts are listened to through the use of digital technologies. Importantly, with the exception of those sounds that are entirely computer-generated, audio is in itself a purely analogue phenomenon. The sound that goes into a microphone at one end and comes out of a speaker at the other is, by definition, an analogue event: a sound wave – a vibration in the air. Everything that happens in between those two instances is a process of translation from one form to another and back again: electrical signals, digital encoding and decoding, transmission through the electromagnetic spectrum, reception by antennae, conversion back into electrical impulses and then, finally, vibration in the air again. In the digital age, then, the simplest path of an audio signal from microphone to listener, in an over-the-air radio context (regardless of whether that is an analogue or a digital radio station), tends to be as follows: analogue, digital, analogue, digital, analogue – or, respectively, sound waves, production technology, distribution technology, reception technology, sound waves.

Of course, even though the waves in the electromagnetic spectrum are themselves fundamentally analogue regardless of the material being broadcast, it is the case that the prevailing technologies of radio distribution have undergone profound changes over the past two decades, and digital transmission formats such as Eureka 147 DAB, HD Radio, and Digital Radio Mondiale have joined the familiar AM and FM, and so have the two embedded digital information systems – RDS and RBDS – that enable stations to send text information within existing AM and FM broadcasts. These services make up the majority of the terrestrial distribution part of the digital radio broadcasting ecology. There are, of course, other methods of digital radio distribution that are not terrestrial, over the air, and these allow for differently configured audience patterns, opportunities for a greater array of programming choices, new and sometimes experimental revenue models for radio business, alternative philosophies underpinning the purpose of radio broadcasting – and so on.

> The original vision of radio's digital future was also based on an assumption that there would be a new dedicated digital platform for radio with some additional features, but the medium as a whole would basically remain the same. It is now clear that this vision was too simplified and optimistic: on the contrary, digitalization has challenged the traditions of radio. (Ala-Fossi et al. 2008: 7)

The internet (particularly, though by no means exclusively, the World Wide Web) has opened up new opportunities for the distribution of programming content, and in so doing it has altered the radio landscape by providing the mechanism and affordances for the addition of live streams, podcasts, downloads and interactive radio services. Satellite radio has opened up ways of broadcasting to much larger geographic areas and has introduced a paid subscription business model to an industry that previously had no technological means of restricting or unlocking its content. As Lessig (2006: 1) has pointed out, with digital technologies, 'code is law'. In other words, the parameters within which the content may be used can be written into the architecture of the software and hardware code itself. In some digital transmission systems, that architecture can even be updated with new code, which is carried in the distributed content. Firmware upgrades for radio receivers may be contained in the distributed radio programming.

Code is law: the means by which radio can be received and listened to can be restricted or enabled through digital means. The ability to prevent listenership unless a monthly payment has been received is not an affordance of analogue broadcasting technologies, and so the digital environment not only changes the means of production, distribution and reception, but also shapes the available technologies of control – and therefore the economic (and, consequently, the political) context for radio broadcasting.

In the meantime, the devices through which we listen to radio programming and to radiophonic content have massively diversified, too – and the platforms through which we consume digitalised radio (in its broadest sense) range from telephones to televisions, from car stereos to networked home audio systems, from desktop computers to tablets. These may be the kinds of technological shifts that we, as radio consumers, notice and pay attention to in the first place, as they are the ones that impact most directly upon our day-to-day media choices, consumer electronics purchasing decisions and the general public discourse about radio in the digital age. However, it's also important to pay attention to the changes, perhaps less visible but by no means less profound, wrought by digital technologies in the workplaces of radio stations themselves; to the change in the practice of radio making and in the roles performed by radio professionals; and especially to the increasing accessibility and affordability of recording and radio production equipment, tools and techniques among non-professionals.

In addition, digital technologies have played a significant role in the stations' ability to syndicate content, to create regional advertising breakouts, and to deploy on-air staff across multiple brands and stations – sometimes simultaneously. Perhaps the most significant technological development that has reshaped the practices and texts of radio broadcasting institutions has been the emergence and refinement of scheduling software for music and other on-air elements such as commercials and station identification jingles. As well as the impact on the content and workflow of the on-air station output, scheduling software's automated processes tend to be fully integrated into a wide range of radio station processes, including administrative reporting and billing systems. Arguably, there is no realm within radio in the digital age – no discursive category – that is unchanged by technological shift. Although both analogue and digital technologies are used in radio today, the overall ecosystem is one that is characterised by its 'digital-ness'. It is the age – rather than each individual piece of radio technology – that is digital.

DAB, HD, Satellite

Inevitably, a book about radio in the digital age must eventually address what is commonly simply referred to as 'digital radio'. Allocutionary broadcasts that send digitally encoded audio signals over the air take a number of different forms, and the differences between them are perhaps more worthy of our attention than the similarities. It is evident to any casual observer that digital radio – whether DAB in Europe, HD radio or satellite radio in the US – follows a model that is in many ways similar to that of analogue (AM/FM) broadcasting. In terms of communicative architecture, a digital radio station follows many of the same conventions as an analogue one. Typically the day will tend to be divided into regular shows; the distribution is time-bound, linear and geographically based; and the audience is targeted through a combination of music and speech elements that appeal to a particular demo- graphic or psychographic profile. That is to say, digital radio broadcasting differs little in form and content from analogue radio broadcasting. However, the affordances of the transmission methodology do allow for some important distinctions, variations and opportunities for new types of programming, audience con- struction and ways of creating cultural meanings.

DAB (digital audio broadcasting) is the label given to the system of digital radio transmission currently in use, and used by over 1,000 radio stations in over 30 countries worldwide – including Australia, China, the United Kingdom, much of Europe and most of Scandinavia (Finland's DAB service was closed down in 2010). The technical standard was the result of a European research project undertaken in the 1980s (O'Neill 2009), which was primarily an exercise in closing what was perceived as 'the analogue gap'. In other words, the discourse around the development of DAB was largely centred on the tech- nologically deterministic, historical inevitability of a completely digital broadcasting landscape. That is, DAB came neither from an industry's commercially driven or public service-led enthusiasm for the benefits of digital radio nor from a consumer demand for improved services, but rather from a political will to move all communications services to a digital platform – and for largely ideological (though also commercial) reasons. In the case of DAB, one strong motivating factor was the desire to shut down analogue terrestrial broadcasts on the AM and FM band (as well as analogue television services) in order to free up broadcasting spectrum that could then be reallocated (and re-sold) to other services. Digital radio is seen as a more efficient use of scarce spectrum resources, and, with a rapid expansion of both supply and demand for mobile services that use the electromagnetic spectrum, the vacation of what is considered to be the prime real estate was seen as a political priority. The Office of Communications (OfCom) in Britain put this proposition somewhat more delicately:

> at some point over the next 10–15 years there may come a point where the vast majority of radio listening is via digital platforms and there may be greater value for consumers in using the VHF Band II [FM] spectrum for other things, rather than simulcasting the services also available on digital. (OfCom 2006: 37, quoted in Ala-Fossi et al. 2008: 7)

Although the development of the Eureka-147 DAB standard as a replacement for AM/FM broadcasting was a European initiative, it has been implemented unevenly across European states because of political, infrastructural and broadcasting industry differences. The history of the development of the technical format, as well as of the bureaucracy that accompanied it behind the scenes, has been catalogued in some depth in other places (see in particular Lax et al. 2008, O'Neill 2009, Rudin 2006, Stoller 2012), and it would be an exercise in redundancy to rehearse that history here. Suffice to say that the path to digital switchover for radio in the UK and Europe has not been smooth and, at the time of writing, the ecology of radio broadcasting is very much characterised by hybridity. There is still, it seems, a political will to shut down the FM band, but neither the consumer nor the industry uptake required to make that a viable option are available.

According to the BBC's website, there are four key improve-
ments to the radio experience introduced by terrestrial DAB.
These are (1) an expansion of services; (2) ease of tuning; (3)
better reception without interference; and (4) the addition of
extra information on a screen. The ability to carry more (and
therefore new) radio stations via the Eureka 147 digital radio
format is created by multiplexing – that is, by multiple channels being carried on a single digital frequency. With the 'better
reception' advantage, care is taken not to go so far as to actually
promise increased sound quality, since in practice the number
of stations on a single multiplex has reduced the available
bandwidth to the point where the audio fidelity of almost all
British DAB stations is lower than that of FM. Better reception
means lack of background noise and interference rather than an
increase in sound quality – and it certainly does not mean the
'CD-quality audio' promised in early promotional material for
the DAB format. The 'ease of tuning' benefit appears to overlook
similar innovations in the digital tuners and memory settings
available within contemporary AM and FM radio receivers, and
the extra information on screen seems merely to duplicate the
kind of information already available to FM radio listeners who
have RDS (radio data system) capabilities in their existing radio.

The British government launched a Digital Radio Action Plan
in 2010, and OfCom was asked to report on both the consumer
takeup and the availability of DAB services across the United
Kingdom. The Action Plan stipulates that 'digital radio switchover should begin only when the market is ready and that it
should be predominantly consumer-led' (OfCom 2012). A target
date of 2015 has been set for digital radio switchover, but the following criteria, rather than the target date, will take precedence
in the matter of deciding to shut down analogue services. These
services will or may be shut, namely,

- when 50% of all radio listening is via digital platforms; and
- when national DAB coverage is comparable to FM, and local
  DAB reaches 90% of the population and all major roads (ibid.)

Other than the intangible benefit of owning modern equipment that is desirable for its sheer newness, aesthetic design
and 'digital-ness', the advantages of DAB seem, from the consumer's perspective, to lie primarily in the diversity of offerings.
British nationwide digital-only stations such as BBC 6Music,
1Xtra, Gaydar Radio, Heat Radio, and NME Radio join stations
that are broadcast on AM or FM locally or only in a couple of
cities but are syndicated nationally on digital channels – such
as Choice FM, Kerrang, XFM, Kiss and Magic – providing
not only additional stations but also additional reach to existing ones, to give a wider audience a greater array of listening
choice.

> Few countries have developed significant levels of DAB services
> over the years and the United Kingdom, while not alone in
> Europe in running DAB services, remains the most advanced
> digital radio landscape in terms of signal coverage, receiver
> take-up and numbers of digital stations. (Lax 2011: 146)

While DAB has been in operation in the UK for well over
a decade, takeup has been more cautious elsewhere. The
switchover to digital radio brings with it some technological
complications, particularly outside of Europe, where for the most
part DAB broadcasts on the L-Band range of frequencies. This
area of the spectrum would likely be problematic for a place like
New Zealand, where the mountainous terrain has caused problems for radio broadcasters since the development of FM radio.
High frequencies are more directional than low frequencies
and therefore need line-of-sight propagation to the transmitter
in order to provide a reliable signal to the reception equipment.
FM signals are broadcast at a higher frequency than AM signals
and thus require high masts in order to achieve this reliable
line-of-sight coverage. Digital broadcasts are carried on a much
higher frequency again. Where FM signals tend to range from
88 to 107 mHz, the L-Band spectrum lies between 1,460 and
1,490 mHz (Ministry of Economic Development 2001). Eureka
147 is designed to operate in frequency ranges around 200 mHz

(VHF) or 1.4G Hz (L-Band). The lower VHF frequencies are used by DAB services in the UK and are less directional, and therefore more robust and resilient in challenging terrain than the L-Band alternative. However, right up until September 2012, terrestrial analogue television was broadcast on the VHF band in New Zealand; hence, to have adopted DAB as a platform for digital radio any earlier, New Zealand would have had to adopt the (unsuitable) European standard. As it is, would-be digital radio broadcasters have had to wait for television to completely migrate to digital platforms before accessing the preferable 200 mHz band. In the meantime DAB technology has moved forward, and the more advanced DAB+ features the capacity for better audio fidelity at higher data compression ratios (lower bit rates) and the ability to carry firmware upgrades to receivers over the air (that is, the ability of actually re-coding the physical devices, so that they may be upgraded simply by tuning in). Countries like Australia, which adopted the DAB platform in more recent years, have tended to adopt the DAB+ format; this format features advanced audio coding (AAC+), which allows for a much higher perceived audio fidelity, using lower bit rates, than the DAB format (currently more common but increasingly out of date).

Due in part to this seemingly rapid process of format redundancy and replacement, there is some resistance from many commercial broadcasters to move forward quickly into digital broadcasting, as this is seen as a largely unnecessary, expensive and high-risk endeavour. But even more off-putting is the risk that an adopted format might quickly become obsolete; this is a concern expressed by members of the New Zealand radio industry, whose resistance to UK-style terrestrial DAB echoes that of many broadcasters within the United States:

> The chief complaint voiced by industry insiders has been that the Eureka system, which relies on the allocation of new portions of the electromagnetic spectrum, would bring new broadcasters into direct competition with existing commercial operators. (McCauley 2002: 509)

To combat this effect, incumbent (primarily commercial) broadcasters in the United States have adopted another form of terrestrial digital radio transmission. HD Radio is the brand name of Ibiquity's proprietary system for in-band, on-channel (IBOC) digital broadcasting – a method of transmitting digital signals on existing AM/FM radio stations. At present, HD Radio is the only digital broadcasting methodology authorised by the FCC for terrestrial radio in the United States of America. The digital signal carried over the air with the existing analogue broadcast can typically carry up to three separate channels of audio data, audio quality and data compression ratio trade-offs being made for each additional digital channel added to the stream. A limitation (or, depending on your viewpoint, an advantage) of this technology is that it restricts the uptake of the broadcast technology to stations already broadcasting and does not open up extra spectrum for new entrants. Rather than adding additional channels for newcomers to the broadcasting space, the spectrum used is identical to that of the current allocation on the AM and FM band.

> The powerful National Association of Broadcasters (NAB) trade association advocated adoption of the In-Band On-Channel (IBOC) system, in the face of considerable engineering evidence that Eureka 147 was technologically superior ... and demonstrate that technological diffusion may depend largely on what causes the least disruption to existing industrial structures. Put another way, the case of IBOC may be seen as an American attempt to make an omelet without breaking the eggs. (Ala-Fossi and Stavitsky 2003: 63)

Unlike DAB radio in Britain, existing broadcasters simply upgrade their transmitters to accommodate the new HD digital signal. Often a radio station will simulcast its existing analogue broadcast output on the first of these digital channels (HD1), and it may offer alternative programming on the other channels (HD2 and HD3). That said, it is possible – and certainly not uncommon – for commercial radio stations to allocate or sublet the additional HD channels to non-profit or community broadcasters.

According to the Ibiquity website, 'there are more than 2,100 stations serving local markets across the country with HD Radio Broadcast Technology' (Ibiquity Digital 2012) and 'more than 1400 HD2/HD3 channels . . . providing consumers more diverse listening options than ever' (ibid). According to figures released by the FCC, at the end of 2009 there were 14,420 radio stations broadcasting in the United States (Riismandel 2010). Even with takeup of one radio station a day, as the Ibiquity website suggests, the market penetration of HD Radio is far from absolute. However, perhaps even more problematically from the perspective of radio broadcasters wishing to reach audiences by using digital technologies, the consumer takeup of HD Radio receivers is very low. Because the technology is a proprietary one, a licence must be purchased from Ibiquity in order to manufacture a receiver. While it is easy to purchase an AM/FM receiver for less than $5, digital receivers typically retail for $50 and more. In addition, because the digital broadcasts take place in the same spectrum – indeed, on the same frequencies – as the analogue broadcast, there is no analogue switch-off date for American radio – as in Britain, across Europe and in many other nations around the world.

In addition to DAB and HD Radio, a third significant digital radio broadcasting format has emerged, flourished and significantly diminished over the twenty years of digital radio history. Among the digital radio ecology that includes (or at least overlaps with) streaming media via the internet, podcasting, music-on-demand services such as Spotify, Deezer and Rdio, or digital music 'serendipity engines' such as Last.fm and Pandora lies the third main digital radio (allocutionary) broadcasting platform: satellite radio. It is significant that the NAB's success in excluding all but radio's incumbents from the realm of terrestrial digital broadcasting opened up a significant commercial opportunity in an area of radio broadcasting over which NAB had no influence. It is equally significant that no commercial satellite radio operators exist in Europe, where DAB allowed for a managed introduction of new services to the broadcasting milieu.

Satellite radio is much like satellite television in terms of its technological architecture and implementation. Upon purchase of a satellite-capable receiver, multiple digital channels can be accessed through paid subscription. Listeners select from a wide choice of radio channels, broadcast via a transmitter on a satellite in geostationary orbit above the reception area. The satellite as a point of origin or source of the broadcast all but eliminates the line-of-sight reception issues introduced by high frequency transmission (other than in extreme meteorological circumstances) and allows for a very broad coverage area, such that it is theoretically possible to be tuned to a single station and drive from Los Angeles to New York without interruption in transmission.

In addition to the hardware-based digital receivers, subscribers are also able to use their passwords to access the radio content online in a number of different ways, by streaming through the website and through a range of mobile and smartphone applications. As well as providing another technological mechanism for reaching audiences across a range of platforms, the streaming content addresses the technological issue of mutual incompatibility between the two satellite distribution services in the United States, Sirius Radio and XM, which started as competitors but are now the same company. A single subscription permits listeners to hear the broadcasts that currently operate on both platforms; but, although hybrid receivers capable of tuning into both Sirius and XM channels are now being manufactured, legacy devices can only receive one or the other. The technological incompatibility is problematic for the broadcasting organisation as well, because it extends not only to the kind of receiver that can pick up Sirius or XM channels (one, but not the other), but also to the satellite distribution methodology itself. At the time of writing, the space hardware that broadcasts XM channels is incapable of broadcasting Sirius channels, and vice versa.

Convergence and Divergence

Satellite radio provides a good case study (by which I mean a problematic and complex one) for exploring the notion of 'convergence', on which much discourse about the digitalisation of media centres. Convergence is often deployed as a technologically deterministic concept, which suggests that the tendency of media technologies in the digital age is to combine and gravitate towards a single distribution channel or media device. A good case can certainly be made for convergence as a genuine phenomenon; for example, through an ecology of applications, smartphones constitute an almost universal device for media consumption, creation and distribution. However, there are also plenty of counter-examples, which serve to re-position convergence as just one out of the many and varied socially (and industrially) negotiated responses to an array of technological affordances in a complex and discursive media environment.

In fact, in the realm of radio broadcasting, evidence of convergence is scant. The ideals of interoperability, open platforms, and universal or even multi-use devices, which would be the hallmarks of a convergent technological ecosystem, seem to be unusual for radio. And, while different types of radio content can be found across a range of different but convergent devices, the inverse is not true. That is to say, you are currently far more likely to be able to listen to the radio on a telephone than you are to be able to make phone calls on a radio. I would argue that currently radio follows instead a divergent path.

For the most part, radio production processes are, at least conceptually, coherent as a broadly standardised form. Technological production processes are used to marry voice, music and sound effect so as to create a text that can operate within almost any radio environment and is freely interchangeable across those different contexts. You can make a radio programme that can be broadcast on FM radio, streaming online, downloadable as a podcast, and distributed via DAB or satellite. The text is platform agnostic. However, the distribution and consumption methodologies for that radio text are not so freely interchange-able. A DAB broadcast may not be received by a smartphone without a DAB chip; an mp3 received via an RSS media enclo-sure through subscription in iTunes may not easily be listened to on the kitchen benchtop radio; a car stereo will typically not receive a live webstream. At present, then, radio consumption exists in a series of silos. This is neither something caused by digital technologies nor a necessary condition of radio in the digital media environment. Indeed the fact that the array of consumer electronics solutions and format choices for radio broadcasting (not to mention consumer uptake of these formats) has led to a divergent set of technological conditions for radio listening does not mean that this is a permanent state of affairs. Indeed Jørn Jensen, the chief advisor of Norwegian public broad-caster NRK, notes:

> Crucially, digital radio chips are now small enough to fit into tablets and mobile phones, and it's expected that a major manu-facturer of these devices will announce digital radio integration early in the year. The implementation of broadcast digital radio in these mass market multimedia devices will place consider-able emphasis on hybrid content, and so this is likely to be a breakthrough that fundamentally changes the way listeners and broadcast conceive the experience of listening to the radio. (Jensen 2011)

The year that Jensen's predicted convergence was optimistically expected to appear 'early in' was 2012, but it seems that this did not in fact take place. However, the European Broadcasting Union (EBU) has subsequently announced a campaign for all new radio receivers and mobile devices to be fitted with a 'Euro-Chip', which implements the main over-the-air techno-logical standards common across Europe: the different digital broadcasting formats (DAB, DAB+ and DMB), and analogue FM reception as well.

It could be said, then, that, rather than a necessary condition of a media form in a digital environment, convergence is an affordance that is available to producers and consumers of that medium, available for them to make use of by bringing together technologists and developers, consumer electronics manufacturers, broadcast organisations and consumers. 'To this end, the EBU will talk to key stakeholders, such as carmakers, legislators and electronics manufacturers, to spread universal awareness of the huge opportunity that Euro-Chip represents' (Steward 2012). It would appear that, in the European context, at least at an industry policy level, the notion of a degree of universality and interoperability for broadcast methodologies introduces an ideal that is considered worth pursuing. Instead of being a deterministic effect of the digital environment, convergence is a goal to which the radio industry and attendant policy bodies apparently strive. The deliberate incompatibility between commercial satellite radio formats in the United States is a case in which there were seemingly strong competitive reasons not to strive for this goal; and yet that decision has proven to be a costly one to correct in the wake of the merger of the two organisations.

Roll Your Own Radio

Despite the creation of many mutually incompatible digital services, one of the affordances of the digital environment, particularly when it comes to internet media, is the ability to bring together several different technologies in order to accomplish a particular goal. New services and solutions can be made by connecting already existing services in new ways. The website If This Then That (ifttt.com) provides an excellent example of user-created 'mash-ups' of web platforms such as Flickr, Dropbox, Facebook and Soundcloud; of monitored events such as calendars, time and temperature; and of different outputs such as email, SMS and phone calls, used to create a programmable series of conditional actions. The site highlights the interoperability of many web platforms and the use of APIs (application programming interfaces) for each service in order to be able to innovate through the connection of useful data and processes. In this way web services may build hybrid tools that go beyond what might be possible or useful, if the service created was custom-built and entirely proprietary (such as a satellite radio service), or restricted to a single environment (such as an iTunes-only radio stream).

A good example of the 'kitset' use of technologies and services that open APIs enable is the Brussels-based internet radio station Laid Back Radio. Laid Back (also known as LDBK) started life in 2002, as a weekly show on a local FM radio station; but it developed into a series of projects under that brand, and the projects include a streaming music programme featuring urban music (jazz, funk, soul, hip hop and more). The stream is, in itself, a simple continuous mix of music with station identifications recorded by DJs and recording artists; but the manner in which that station is delivered makes it differ from many of its contemporaries in simple but important ways, which demonstrate a consideration of and an adaptation to the affordances of the digital environment. From the station's website, listeners are encouraged to download a desktop or a mobile application. The player begins the stream upon launch, but also loads track information, artist biography and images from Last.fm through its application programming interface. The wiki-based data from Last.fm is imported and displayed in the player, alongside a stream of updates about and by the radio station on Twitter. Using a sign-in section in preferences, the station will also 'scrobble' track plays to the listener's Last.fm account, thereby keeping a record and aggregating data from the time spent listening live. There is no 'listen again' feature, no audio on demand or podcast availability within the application itself, though DJ mixes are posted to a third-party service, Mixcloud, and this provides the station with another platform on which to find listeners. However, the simple collection of services rolled into one adds data from more than one source (the station music database and the Last.fm database) and exports data to more than one source (the Twitter and Last.fm accounts of individual application users).

Of course, APIs are created and made available by web companies that are themselves operating in a commercial environment, and so the challenge to balance the usefulness of their service in a range of unforeseeable and innovative contexts with the desire to maintain control over the uses and applications of that service is a difficult one. At the time of writing, the hybrid, kitset Laid Back player is currently inoperable due to some changes in the data architecture of some of the services it uses, and the organisation is considering fundraising options in order to rebuild and reconfigure its player so that these integrated functions may work once again.

Technology and Perception

The experience of the listener is at the centre of the challenge facing research and development engineers and digital technologists who work at the vanguard of audio media technologies. For instance, within the BBC's research and development (R&D) unit, the focus for audio researchers is not on radio per se, but on sound as it relates to all media content, whether attached to video or visual media or by itself, as an audio-only piece of communication. However, considerations about how that audio content works are also very different in a range of different contexts – and for many different reasons. Rather than design for a convergence of any kind, technologists grapple with the diversification of media content, platforms and devices and must invent technological solutions that address the challenges of data transfer and medium specificity as well as the potential of different contexts for the consumption and interaction of a particular kind of media content.

For the 2012 Wimbledon tennis championships, BBC Radio 5 Live introduced NetMix, an online tool that enabled audiences to control individually the volume of courtside microphones and of live audience applause in relation to the BBC's own audio commentary. In the *Telegraph* newspaper, Robert Brun, the head of technology for the BBC's Audio and Music Department, explained the motivation and context for this technological development and specific implementation:

> The BBC receives lots of complaints from the public regarding sound balance – with many of them wanting the sound of the commentators turned up and the noise for a match turned down. Wimbledon was a clear choice to launch this product for as there are always so many comments about the amount of grunting from the players. (Barnett 2012)

Apart from elements of simple personalisation, researchers are exploring ideas of experiential quality and acoustic 'immersion'. Indeed, some of the audio research being developed at the BBC R&D division in Salford is on fully immersive surround audio, which factors in not just width of field but also height and navigable depth (that is, an acoustic space that may actually be walked through rather than simply observed by a stationary listener). To accomplish this technical feat – fully immersive, 3-dimensional audio – the researchers developed a 22.2 surround sound system and put up an audio-only drama production in order to demonstrate the system's possibilities. However, in the context of radio, there are perhaps both limited numbers of broadcast texts that would be suited for a 22.2 surround experience and limited numbers of listening contexts that would warrant such an impressive sound system installation. At a presentation about this technology and its implementation at the BBC, I interviewed research engineer Anthony Churnside about the possibilities and the difficulties inherent in this ambitious, immersive radiophonic experience.

Of course, one of the key challenges of transmtting complex media information that needs to be spread over so many separate channels is the amount of data required to capture and represent all of those individual audio streams. Particularly within the context of radio broadcasting, the extent to which that raises technical challenges at the upper limit of bandwidth also brings up the need for these sorts of audio media services to be made available at all. But this redundancy can be addressed, and bandwidth requirements for audio are not fixed by the affordances of the digital media technologies, as Churnside explains.

It depends on how it's managed. There is no point in us carrying redundant data. How you represent those 22.2 channels in a data stream is what's important, as it's unlikely that it will be 24 linear, PCM audio channels, because that, I would guess, would carry a lot of redundant data. (Churnside 2012)

Other than through simple data compression, it is possible to address the problem of redundant audio data by altering the way in which one approaches the fundamental broadcast paradigm of a channel (or group of channels) of audio continuously streaming. Churnside and his colleagues are approaching this potential problem of data transfer in the radio and audio media context by adopting approaches from other media forms that take advantage of certain affordances of the digital technologies.

We are working out if we can represent the sound experience as a series of objects rather than as a series of channels. The way some computer games deal with audio is that they have a box of assets and each of those assets represents an audio object or part of an audio object, and then there is an engine within the computer game that pieces those together, plays them out at the right time. What I'm thinking about is 'can we take an approach to broadcasting that is inspired by that model of breaking down a sound scene into component parts and treating each of those parts in terms of its perceptual importance to the listener. So, treating sounds that are foreground as more important – they will take up more data and space – than sounds that are diffuse (reverb and so on) and sounds going on in the background. (ibid.)

And, likewise, there will be many radio texts that simply do not have the requirement for an immersive and high-definition representation within a surround sound environment, yet they must – if these environments are to exist – be at least able to be experienced satisfactorily in those contexts. As discussed in chapter 3, there is much radio content that is typically experienced while one is doing the other things that make up daily life. The device that we call the radio on the kitchen bench provides a source of information and entertainment that is environmental, certainly, but it need not be entirely immersive, and certainly not all-consuming. As a result, there are significant data transmission savings that can be made even in transmission to a system capable of reproducing full, three-dimensional surround sound.

> The audio data to produce, say, the *Today Programme*, which has two or three speakers [is comparatively low] and to carry that as 22.2 discrete channels would be a rather inefficient way of delivering that programme. (ibid.)

And while total, three-dimensional sonic immersion might not represent a significant improvement in listening experience by comparison with the gratifications an audience might derive from the *Today Programme*, there are conceivably other types of programming, such as drama, sport and musical live events, for which such immersion might provide a clear experiential point of difference. Of course, the requirement to have the necessary equipment installed in one's preferred listening space is one consideration, as is the extent to which it is important where one is situated within that listening space.

> Learning from television, there's a gradual move from stereo to 5.1 which has a single centre speaker at the front and the reason for that is because it accompanies the screen and it allows you to widen the sweet spot so sounds can still come from the centre when you're sitting on the edges of the sweet spot. Whereas radio has no screen, so there are questions as to whether that centre speaker is as important for radio, audio-only or what-have-you. (ibid.)

With respect to the context in which people might listen to such immersive radio experiences, the possibilities are greater than one might at first imagine – especially in of what has long been thought of as one of radio's most significant listening environments: the car. Churnside explains:

> A car is a very controlled environment acoustically – particularly a modern car, and especially one with a silent electric engine. So the environment of your car might be more controllable than the sound system of your living room. When the car is built, the sound system is designed for the interior of that car. The parameters are nailed down and fixed. So you can do quite a lot

> with how you want to design the sound system and place the speakers. A living room is quite a different story. (ibid.)

However, there are far less conducive environments and platforms with which to listen to audio content, and to treat those environments in the same way as the acoustically treated 'silent car' environment not only makes little sense in terms of the sheer weight of redundant data that would necessarily be transmitted, but the sound of the output would require different treatment simply in order to be experienced at all. For instance, it is possible to listen to audio from a tablet computer without headphones plugged into it. In that instance, prioritising audio fidelity is counter-productive, as a high dynamic range (and therefore low average loudness) stream would conceivably be lost, especially in a noisy environment. The different content and contexts for radio and audio listening and the divergent nature of the different platforms and environments in which that listening takes place raise questions about whether audio should be treated or mastered differently for different devices; whether that mastering could perhaps be performed locally on those different devices – and so on. An FM radio will receive and replicate whatever is sent to it. If the 22.2 surround radio drama is broadcast over some digital distribution channel, is it important that something with only a single speaker is even capable of receiving those 24 channels? And to what extent should that decision be made at the point of production, encoding, distribution or reception? According to Churnside, 'these are all things we're looking at and there are lots of things to solve' (ibid.).

As the developments in audio and radio become rapidly more sophisticated and the affordances of digital technology are explored and experimented with in greater depth, the simple skeuomorphic approach of putting audio tape on a screen to be cut up by clicking a mouse rather than by wielding a razor blade is replaced by one containing some technological feats that are native to that digital environment. The environment offers us the potential for genuine innovation within the space, instead of us modelling some older function. A simple example of this feature is the RCS music programming software GSelector, which uses a series of programming 'goals' (hence the 'G') rather than the longstanding practice of using categories and rotates within and across those categories in order to achieve particular music programming ends. Because the goals are the result of a series of preferences for which algorithms can be calculated, the 'index cards in boxes' metaphor for choosing which record should be played next can be abandoned in favour of a more 'digitally intuitive' method, which does not seek merely to emulate the affordances of an analogue, electric age world of broadcasting.

CHAPTER SEVEN

Radio in Society

Introduction

The way in which radio as we know it works today has come about as the result of a series of historical settlements that have been arrived at in order for certain political and social goals to be met. In response to those settlements, innovations of techne (that is, the tools, techniques, and art and craft of radio) have been developed, at least in part, to further those goals within the parameters of the affordances of the technological environment and within the restrictions of the technologies of control that arise from those settlements. Radio is not simply a business; nor is it just a medium for entertainment – though it is of course these things too. But the fact that it is these things is subordinate to (or rather in the service of) the medium's role in society and the purpose to which it has been put by policy-makers over time.

In addition, radio plays a role with respect to furthering democratic principles and building and reinforcing communities: it acts as a site of activism and political struggle, and also as a tool for development. As radio has been traditionally defined and institutionalised at the level of the nation state, ideas about its manifestation as a community focal point differ from country to country. The UK is in the process of reimagining and developing its community radio sector; the USA has a tradition of local public radio and student broadcasting, and is (at the time of writing) in the process of establishing laws that would authorise and facilitate an entire ecology of low-power FM community radio stations across the country; in Australia, with its vastly dispersed rural population, community radio has become a powerful and popular cultural force; in New Zealand, much of the community radio is organised around an access model, with a broad range of diverse communities within a single geographic location having equal access to the airwaves; while in some other countries community radio simply does not exist in a recognisable form and there are instances of activism involving unauthorised community radio stations being set up in areas where free speech is discouraged. But, while there are significant differences between different national approaches to community radio, the ways in which the medium of radio relates to these communities are also undergoing significant change within the shifting media environment.

Likewise, the opportunities for radio to be used as a tool for development are altered and perhaps amplified by changes in technologies. The use of radio in the spread of agricultural knowledge and health education to communities in Africa and beyond is a significant instance of the social good that radio can provide as a medium of communication and of the extent to which both practices such as podcasting or archiving for on-demand listening and the ability to make reports through the mobile phone, which is now almost entirely ubiquitous, have amplified and extended the reach and impact of these services. In addition, 'pirate' and unauthorised broadcasting, while still phenomena that take place over the FM airwaves, have adapted to the digital environment, extending their reach and interacting with audiences in new ways.

The potential for radio as a social tool in the digital age exists in a context that also includes a parallel rise of mobile telephony, the potential integration of open wireless networks into a community mesh, and social media and information networks that connect communities online. At the same time, the context within which all radio broadcasting takes place – whether for community, commercial, public or other ends – is inscribed by political and economic as well as technological factors, and these factors yield both affordances and tensions within that ecology. Political responses to the technological environment must be realistic with respect to economic restraints. Technological opportunities that respond to the political environment may have profound commercial possibilities. The economics of radio within a specific political environment are subject to the technological environment. These factors push and pull on each other, and so a profound change to any one of them potentially affects all three of them – politics, technology and economics – while remaining dependent upon, and ultimately responsive to, the other two factors.

As Tim Wall (2005) has shown, the political economy of internet radio is in many ways profoundly different from, indeed almost antithetical to, the political economy of traditional radio, broadcast 'over the air'. The technologies of distribution used by the two types of broadcasting are central to these differences: over-the-air radio stations are very expensive to set up (high fixed costs), though the cost of an additional listener is negligible (low marginal costs) and exists within a highly regulated and restricted context with a high degree of scarcity of spectrum; in contrast, a streaming internet radio station can be very cheap to set up (low fixed costs), but the cost of each additional listener is cumulative in terms of bandwidth and distribution (high marginal costs) and exists within a very unregulated context, with no degree of 'spectrum' scarcity whatsoever. There is always room for one more streaming radio station on the internet and, as long as not too many people are listening, it can be very inexpensive to establish. It is important to understand the social, political, economic and media-ecological context of radio in order to draw a full picture of why radio is the way it is and of the ways it changes by moving from one media environment to another. As Wall explains, 'if attention to technology is insufficient to understand over-the-air radio it is likely to be insufficient to understand internet music radio' (2005: 31).

The ways in which the economics of radio station ownership, management and production operate shift in relation to the technological environment as well. The professional practice of radio is subject to the same kinds of technology-led efficiencies that are prevalent across the media and communications industries.

> The labor of communication workers is also being commodified as wage labor has grown in significance throughout the media workplace. In order to cut the labor bill and expand revenue, managers replaced mechanical with electronic systems to eliminate thousands of jobs in the printing industry as electronic typesetting did away with the jobs of linotype operators. Today's digital systems allow companies to expand this process. (Mosco 2009: 13)

In order to understand radio in the digital age, it is important, then, to understand not only the affordances of the technologies, but also the ends to which the medium is to be put, as well as the political and economic framework that both define and restrict the efficacies of those purposes and interventions – and ultimately to understand the changing nature of those tensions, so that new and positive interventions may be imagined that accommodate and maximise the benefits offered by the changes.

The Political Economy of Radio

The political economy of radio describes the set of economic, infrastructural and legal parameters within which radio is made, distributed and consumed, and is also a system of technologies of control. Mosco (1996: 2) describes political economy as 'the study of the social relations, particularly the power relations, that mutually constitute the production, distribution, and consumption of resources'.

To discuss radio within the context of the digital age is therefore necessarily to examine what is allowed and what is restricted through the application of policy and through the affordances and effectivities of that system. The key to understanding the political economy of radio is to consider that the way in which radio is organised is neither a natural nor an essential response to the technological form of radio, but rather a series of settlements that have been arrived at and negotiated over time, for a range of different purposes.

For instance, historically speaking – and indeed to this day – radio broadcasting is not only controlled but also largely organised at the level of the nation state. The widely held idea that radio is a primarily (and importantly) local phenomenon has some basis in the implementation of individual radio stations and in the texts that these stations may broadcast – for instance local weather or news. However, that view overlooks the extent to which radio is not local or even regional at all, but it is instead far more commonly owned and operated – as well as regulated – at a national level. But, just as localism is not a product of the onto-logical parameters of radio, it is not because of the technological characteristics of the medium that the institutional form of radio is nationally configured. The technology certainly allows for that particular form of organisation, but it does not insist on it. Radio transmission technologies are in themselves unaffected by the technologies of cartography. The boundary of a nation state does not affect the transmission of a radio signal. Rather the laws of a nation state affect the ways in which a radio signal may be estab-lished and the purposes to which it may be deployed. Those laws are agreements between groups of people (generally people with power), codified and then enforced. They are neither inevitable nor unchangeable, but, once set in place, they provide a system of restrictions and controls that act upon the media environment and shape the range of possibilities in terms of the ways in which actors can make use of the affordances of that technological environment.

For this reason, the new affordances of the digital envi-ronment introduce new challenges to the assumptions and assertions underpinning those historical settlements and sys-tems of control. They open new possibilities and complexities within the economic framework of radio (some of which con-tribute to emancipatory and democratising processes within the media landscape while others do not) and affect the political and legislative context in which the medium operates as part of a new 'socio-techno-political' ecology. The starting point for this analysis of the political economy of radio is the underlying observation of the relative stability of the condition and institutional infrastructure of radio towards the end of the electric age and at the beginning of the digital. The political economy approach seeks to understand, and thereby maximise, the potential for a public, social good that is manifest in a series of economic and policy technologies and interventions – such as legislation and patterns of media ownership. The laws surrounding the use of radio broadcasting and the ways in which spectrum is allocated are all but settled and, apart from some differences in detail internationally and a fairly universal drift towards liberalisation and deregulation around the world, no major challenges have been raised to the established fundamentals (such as who may broadcast; the division between public and private radio ownership; how the spectrum is engineered and managed; or even the fact that the electromagnetic spectrum is utilised for allocutionary communication at all).

Most of the agreements and settlements that inscribe the way in which radio works today were made early in the technology's history. Those agreements have been a way of codifying and controlling a series of responses to a broad range of affordances, brought about by an electric age media ground. Specific technologies such as transmitters, broadcast studios, relay stations and receivers; institutional practices and conventions such as breakfast shows, news bulletins, station identification and ad breaks; and ownership patterns and ideas about the function of public broadcasting – all stem from the way in which the political economy of radio has been arrived at and settled upon. These are not and have never been 'just the way radio works', but instead radio works that way because that is what has been decided. As Tim Wall explains:

> Radio technology did not become a broadcast form – programming being sent outwards from a central station to mass audiences – until the 1920s, and it had initially been utilised as a point-to-point, reciprocal form of communication. Music

radio developed in the USA from the 1950s (Rothenbuhler and McCourt 2002), and many European state and public broadcasters resisted these changes until the late 1960s and early 1970s (Barnard 1989). (Wall 2012: 336)

The technological environment of the electric age provided the occasion to have the conversations and debates that led to those decisions being made, but the range of affordances offered by the landscape that allows for transmission over the electromagnetic spectrum is far broader than the array of implementations currently in use. In addition, specific technologies are developed in order to make use of (and solve problems arising from) the settlements that have been made. In other words, the discovery of the electromagnetic spectrum did not cause broadcasting, but rather the decision to use broadcasting as a model for the use of the electromagnetic spectrum was arrived at as the result of a desire to meet (and indeed establish) a set of social and cultural practices. Wall (2012) points out, for instance, that it was the social and cultural mobility of young people in the 1950s and the development of post-war commuter culture in US cities, rather than the technology of transistor circuitry, that acted as the key driver of listening on the move. Even though 'the distribution technology is important in enabling expansion or innovation in broadcasting practice, cultural aspiration and use are far more determining' (ibid., p. 337).

But the political economy that made possible the sorts of interventions and agreements that led to the kind of radio with which we were familiar and that we understood at the end of the twentieth century may not necessarily be an appropriate political economy of radio in a changed technological environment. While many of the responses of broadcasting policy-makers and industry leaders have been an attempt to maintain the status quo in the face of a profoundly changed media environment and a broad range of new tensions, the shift from an electric age set of affordances and effectivities to an entirely different set of parameters in the digital age would suggest that the kinds of conversations and debates that led to the current status quo may need to be held again, starting from first principles. Namely: given an understanding of the affordances of the current technological environment and given the potential to innovate within that space for communicative ends, what is the best way to maximise the social good?

The answer settled upon in the time of Lord Reith (in response to the electric age technological environment), and on the strength of which the BBC was established, had to do with ideals about social uplift, the creation of a monopoly mechanism designed to nationalise communication in Britain, and the establishment of an allocutionary framework for a top-down distribution of entertainment, education and information with a foundation in class-based ideologies and morality, as these were the dominant values espoused by those in positions of power, who were able to make these sorts of settlements and agreements.

Later on, decisions about whether some of the functions of broadcasting (in the service of the social, public good) could be better catered by market interventions led to the rise of commercial radio in the UK; but by that time the infrastructure and logic of broadcasting as a response to the technological environment were firmly enshrined within the electric age context.

I argue that the infrastructure, parameters and conventions of radio in the digital age are, as yet, still in the early experimental, pioneering stages. Decisions about the political economy of radio (or indeed communication) within the digital landscape need neither echo nor simply extend the settlements made in response to the electric age environment. Analysis of the affordances of the digital environment from a political economy perspective may reveal alternative paths and offer imaginative and positive ways for policy-makers to intervene meaningfully and for technologists to innovate. However, it seems likely that the kinds of settlements that will be made for radio in the digital age will likewise reflect the dominant set of values espoused by those in positions of power who are able to make these sorts of settlements and agreements today. It also seems likely that these kinds of settlements will inspire a range of different critical and activist responses.

Technologies of Control

One of the primary concerns of legislators in the early days of radio stemmed from a perception of the power of this new technological form. Central to that concern was the ability not simply to communicate, but to persuade over great distances and perhaps spread messages of political dissent or 'immorality'. Therefore systems of control were deemed necessary and put in place in order to ensure that the 'right' people had the ability to broadcast, and the 'wrong' people did not. This system of authorisation – the control over certain patterns of behaviour with respect to what was considered a dangerous medium, and the general discourse of the citizenry – was achieved through the technology of legislation, and also through the mechanism of radio and spectrum allocation. This is, in large part, the reason why we have the radio that we do.

Legislation, however, does not merely attempt to control who may broadcast and to whom, but also many other parameters of radio ownership and radio business. For instance, the broadcasting policy of most nations imposes restrictions over the number of radio stations that can be owned by a single organisation. Many nations also forbid cross-media ownership (preventing, for instance, newspaper owners also to own radio stations, and vice versa); they impose specific conditions about the characteristics and behaviours of the kind of person who might be deemed 'fit and proper' to be allowed to broadcast; and they also impose laws about the foreign ownership of radio companies. There is, of course, a wide range of diversity among such systems of control, from nation to nation, but it is significant that these sorts of legislation exist in every country and that, while they differ in degree, they do not differ in kind. Even in a continent-sized country such as the United States, radio is legislated for at a national rather than a state level.

The fact that radio is, broadly speaking, a national phenomenon does not, of course, mean that it only exists in a national
form – merely that it is primarily controlled and owned at that
level. There are local and regional instances of radio, and even
some hyperlocal low-power FM examples (see Dunbar-Hester
2010). In the UK, the condition under which commercial radio
stations were initially allowed to operate in the 1960s was that
they provide something that the entirely nationally configured
BBC did not offer at that time. The response to that condition
was the establishment of local radio. There are also international
radio stations that broadcast via Shortwave. However, these are,
generally speaking, subject to the technologies of control and to
the power relationships that exist to permit, facilitate or restrict
broadcasting at a national level.

But the prevention of broadcasting is not the purpose of radio
legislation. Rather such legislation exists to ensure that the
powerful technological ground offered by the electromagnetic
spectrum and, more recently, the flow of digital data across a
range of distribution mechanisms serve the public good appropriately. Current dominant political philosophies in Western
nations such as Britain and the US hold that free market
competition solves many (though not all) of the challenges of
maximising the public good through the medium of radio.
As a result, there has been an increasing tendency to encourage private ownership of radio companies and a relaxation of
regulation, in order to facilitate and liberate market solutions
to consumer needs. In 1979 the US government's Federal
Communications Commission identified two primary benefits of
deregulation:

> Producers of goods and services must be responsive to con-
> sumers' desires in order to compete successfully with rival
> producers. Consumers, by their choice of purchases, determine
> which producers will succeed. Moreover, not only does the
> competition among producers for consumers lead to the pro-
> duction of goods and services that consumers most want, the
> same competitive process forces producers continually to seek

> less costly ways of providing those goods and services. (Quoted
> in Head and Sterling 1990: 456)

However, there is, broadly speaking, a recognition that the
market cannot and will not meet all of the needs of a diverse
society, and there are significant niche interests, some minority
concerns, and even entire sectors of the citizenry that are not
addressed and whose needs are not met by an entirely commercial radio broadcasting environment. As a result, public and
community broadcasting offers a range of spaces within which
radio can do more than simply satisfy a desire to gather together
as large an audience as possible, in order for people to be com-
moditised en masse.

Moreover, the growth logic of capitalism among radio station
owners leads to a desire to conglomerate; and the possible range
of choices offered, rather than differentiating so as to cater for
different markets, will tend to converge on a single mass audience (or several large ones). Glasser observed:

> A station will duplicate an existing format [within a market]
> rather than produce a unique format if its share of the audience
> for a duplicated format yields higher profits than the profits
> generated by the entire audience for a unique format. (Glasser
> 1984: 129)

Commercial radio companies seek to expand and aggregate their
ownership of individual stations so as to make savings through
various efficiencies of delivery. As a result anti-monopoly laws
exist, and in most countries further restrictions are placed, so
that the diversity of voices and interests is not compromised
by commercial radio's preference for maximising profit for
shareholders over its desire to provide quality programming that
meets the criteria for achieving the public good.

In New Zealand, where deregulation of the radio industry is
near total, two international corporations own the vast majority of the radio stations around the country (see Rosenberg
and Mollgaard 2010), and each of those stations is virtually the
mirror image of its rival (its counterpart owned by the other

company). The ambition is not to cater for all the interests or serve all the needs, but to take as large a slice as possible of the biggest pies available. Jane Kelsey (1999: 8) explains the ideology behind the deregulation of radio (and many other industries) in New Zealand in the following manner: '"The New Zealand Experiment" – the relentless pursuit of free-market principles that began in 1984 – exposed a small, remote country of 3.8 million people to the full impact of international market forces.'

As a result, every available scrap of the spectrum was put up for commercial tender, all restrictions over cross-media and foreign ownership were removed, and all controls (other than extant laws regarding decency and appropriate libel laws) over what a radio station was allowed to broadcast were dropped. The ensuing proliferation of stations and their subsequent aggregation, and the effect of these phenomena on the radio landscape in New Zealand has been outlined in some detail elsewhere (see Dubber 2007, Shanahan and Duignan 2005, Zanker 1996, Watts 2010). The end result has been a marginalisation and restriction of non-commercial and public broadcasting services; a clear segmentation of large demographic target audiences, broadly divided as they were between very similar offerings from the two competing international companies; and an apparent and growing inability to distinguish between advertising and information – at least on the part of some listeners, who are immersed in a commercially saturated media environment (Watts 2010) in spite of what would appear to be a small but healthy public radio sector, a diverse community and Iwi radio ecosystem, and a seemingly robust and almost completely unregulated low-power FM radio environment, which lies alongside the corporate fare.

Although New Zealand presents an extreme case, the tendency towards deregulation in the industry has emerged as a primary shaper of the way in which the radio industry works at the beginning of the digital age. Tony Stoller's explanation of the path that has led us to the kind of radio we have today emerges from an experience in the British media context; but in general these same principles apply broadly across many Western nations.

> It has all happened within three very different regulatory philosophies for radio broadcasting: the last years of Reithian paternalism; the brief flourishing of a mixed social economy for radio; and the eventual triumph of market liberalism. (Stoller 2012: 150)

The logic of free market forces, construed as a basis for the imposition or removal of technologies of control over the airwaves, has become a more dominant framework for policy-making worldwide than the logic of maximising a public good, although that usually features too, in secondary place. This is not to say that the commercial radio sector is necessarily at odds with the public good. Rather it only serves the public good as a byproduct of its corporate purpose, given a mixed broadcasting ecology, a series of restraints and parameters within which it may work, and a series of checks and balances. In other words, commercial radio has an opportunity rather than a right to profit from its provision of a broader social good, and it is allowed to profit because it is believed that this kind of market incentive meets the political economy agenda most effectively. Although this aspect of the free market approach to broadcasting is often lost under neoliberal rhetoric, the purpose of public and community broadcasting is to deliver further social and public good in those places that commercial radio has no clear incentive to reach, and to provide balances so that commercial broadcasting contributes to the overall ecology without detriment.

The way in which these technologies of control are administered varies again from place to place, but the process generally takes the form of some institutional body overseeing policy development, researching the efficacy of the policies that are already in place, and running the day-to-day application and enforcement of regulations. In the UK, this body is OfCom (the Office of Communications); in the United States, the FCC (Federal Communications Commission). There are some more complex arrangements of national broadcasting policy, however. In New Zealand, for instance, spectrum management and broadcasting policy are the domain of the MED (formerly the Ministry for Economic Development, now the Ministry of Business, Innovation and Employment – although the original acronym has stuck), but the Ministry of Culture and Heritage also has some oversight and advisory roles within that process.

Just as concerns about the potential power of the distribution technologies prompted a series of government interventions and the implementation of a series of controls in the early days of radio, very similar debates concerning the ways in which the internet should be regulated have emerged in recent years. The technological ground is fundamentally different, but the debates revolve around the same sorts of themes – such as who should be allowed access to the internet, what an appropriate configuration of public, private and community use might be, and so on. The underlying rhetoric of serving the public good (or protecting the public good) remains. The degree to which some of those decisions are made at a national level has arguably diminished, though globally centralised control – such as that proposed by the suggestion to include the internet within the United Nations International Telecommunications Union, which was put forward at the UN World Conference on International Telecommunications 2012 – has, to date, not taken effect (this seems unlikely after the bid's rejection at that conference), and nations still have autonomous control over the restrictions and conditions under which their citizens may use the technology.

One current debate at the heart of the political economy of the internet, and one that would have a great deal of influence over the way in which technologies of control would be structured around internet radio (particularly, though by no means exclusively, in the United States), is around the argument over 'net neutrality' vs 'data discrimination'. Telecommunications companies, whose networks make up the data infrastructure that constitutes the digital age equivalent of the electromagnetic spectrum, are largely in corporate rather than state hands. As the cables and networks are essentially private property rather than public assets, the Telecoms wish to prioritise certain types of data (their own, and those of their biggest customers) in order to maximise profits as a result of the use of their infrastructure. In so doing, they wish to replicate in many ways the allocutionary, centralised, one-to-many model of communication in which corporate interests have a voice and private individuals are configured as audience and consumers. That asymmetry of access is an issue of public good, and one that policy-makers must decide. That debate over 'digital spectrum management' has parallels with how the controls over the electromagnetic spectrum for radio broadcasting shaped the ultimate uses to which radio could be put and the ways in which it could be structured. Consequently, legislation and public policy responding to that proposal of internet asymmetry constitute potentially one of the most significant technologies of control that could shape the range of affordances available for communication in the digital age.

Public Broadcasting in the Digital Age

If the role of public broadcasting is merely to address the shortcomings of commercial broadcasters – that is, to meet and address the areas of market failure – then the job is a simple one: analyse those sectors of society whose needs are not being met by current offerings, and supplement in kind: fill in the gaps. However, that very narrow definition of public service media does the sector an injustice. While Hanretty's (2011: 4) broad definition stipulates the social use of the medium, the mechanism through which it is funded, and its relationship to the nation state, Raboy (1995) and others (Banerjee and Seneviratne 2006) describe the role of the public broadcaster in more detail. Issues such as universal accessibility, universal appeal, attention to minorities, distance from commercial and political vested interests, and broad democratic principles delineate the role of the public service broadcaster.

But, as has already been discussed, the notion of broadcasting as a model for media provision of any kind in the digital age is a presupposition with no obvious basis in the affordances of the media environment. In other words, just as there was an opportunity in the age of Lord Reith to make decisions about the way in which radio could be configured – and 'broadcasting' was simply one of the settlements that were made about its implementation – likewise, to suggest that the task of providing media services that promote democratic principles such as inclusion, the development of texts with universal appeal, and attention to minorities must necessarily use an allocutionary model is to misunderstand the potential for innovation and the opportunity for genuine public service via media in the digital age.

Analyses of the ways in which some public broadcasting organisations have met the challenge of digital technologies (for instance in Bonet et al. 2011) reveal two main trends: to envisage the online distribution methodology as either supplementary or analogous to traditional over-the-air radio in an allocutionary mode; and to consider the matter of the device on which the prospective listener will 'tune in' to be a problem solved. In the study of the BBC I conducted with Tim Wall (Wall and Dubber 2009), we identified this way of thinking about the role of radio in the online environment as having a 'broadcast orientation', but we noted that there were also members of the BBC operational teams who have responded to the challenges of the new media environment with what we identified as an 'online interactive' orientation. The two different ways of thinking about the role of public radio from an operational perspective were starkly contrasted: the former – thinking of the internet in terms of a vehicle in which the radio brands could be extended; the latter – thinking of it in terms of a new framework with different communicative possibilities, which might be more readily described as 'many to many' and which could make use of more open, conversational platforms for engagement that have less to do with broadcasting and more to do with public media access. At the time, I remarked (somewhat in jest – but with a serious point) that the corporation should change its name in order to shift its orientation – from the British Broadcasting Corporation to something like BPM: British Public Media. In a policy document for New Zealand on Air, media commentator Russell Brown and I offered the following provocation:

> Broadcasters and publishers must ask 'What is it that we do? What are we good at? Who is our audience? What do they want to do? What can we offer them in that respect? What technologies exist to enable that? How then can we prosper?' rather than simply 'How do we make television, radio and print digital?' (Brown and Dubber 2007)

While the renaming of something as internationally recognisable as the BBC is supremely unlikely, the fundamental shift in thinking that such a thought experiment points to is something that may need to take place anyway, simply because the philosophy of public service media requires rethinking in the context of a new media environment. What exactly is the role of a public service media organisation in the digital age? Are continuities of service as important as discontinuities which introduce new ways of addressing issues such as universal accessibility, universal appeal, attention to minorities, distance from commercial and political vested interests, and broad democratic principles?

Of course, there are already some interesting initiatives underway that recast the BBC's relationship to culture. For instance, the corporation has led a great deal of technological innovation in response to the digital environment, especially with respect to methods of distribution (iPlayer, for instance). Likewise, the corporation has been the site of some cutting-edge and forward thinking ideas about digital archives and the commons, and, in his role as controller of archive development, Tony Ageh has proposed some profound changes in the ways in which not only preservation, but also public access to publicly funded content should be considered in the digital age. Of course, Ageh is far from being alone in the institution in his manner of thinking, but he is significant in terms of penetration into the culture of the corporation because of his position. In a sense, what Ageh signals for the BBC (and for public broadcasters elsewhere) – perhaps not as a template, but certainly as an aspiration – is the opportunity to take on a role of thought leadership when it comes to the political economy of the media: practising public intellectuals and patrons engaged with issues of social good, rather than merely makers of quality programming. For the most part, the primary role of BBC radio staff is to enact an ideology that is made possible by a media environment. The ideology responds to, rather than is imposed by, that media environment (and, of course, the received political economy).

The ideology is neither necessary nor permanent. The media environment has changed.

The digital environment presents challenges as well as opportunities for public media organisations, and the rules of engagement differ on many fronts. As Russell Brown and I observed:

> Digitalisation has meant a great many things for broadcasters, not the least of which has been the destabilisation of the core principle underlying its economic basis: ownership of the means of distribution. The Internet has not only undermined this central principle of broadcasting communication and business, it has now started to work on the broadcasters' monopoly over the creation of content. (Brown and Dubber 2007)

Loss of ownership of the means of distribution means that BBC content now exists within commercial contexts such as YouTube (owned by Google), and it opens up the possibility for commercial competitors to interfere directly with the public's ability to access public broadcasting content – for example, customers of Virgin Media's internet service have complained of a throttling and 'traffic shaping' of bandwidth being specifically applied to BBC iPlayer data. Whether true or not, this is certainly possible. If the broadcasting organisations no longer own the means of distribution and are no longer the sole providers of content, it is important to ask what their role should be – and a return to first principles in order to answer that question seems warranted. Not to ask 'How should public broadcasting adapt to the internet?' but rather: 'If we were inventing public service media now, from scratch, what would it seek to achieve, and how best could it go about achieving that?'

In a very real sense, we are at a new moment in media history, much like the one that faced Reith. There are new opportunities to develop new types of broadcasting – as well as media forms that are less like broadcasting and perhaps more like conversation. The emergence of the digital media ground and the affordances it enables provide the opportunity to seek to enrich the public and social good in brand new ways. Not necessarily ways that replace the old ones, but ways that develop and enhance them and that we may not have thought of, had we not started from first principles and, importantly, from an understanding of the affordances of the media ecology. This is not an opportunity to seek to achieve the same social good using new methods, but an opportunity to do more and better. And perhaps there is also the opportunity, once again, to come up with new solutions to things that can be further developed and added to by commercial interests. Innovation in this respect is positive with respect to competition; it is not anti-competitive.

Radio for and by Communities

Just as the definition of radio is problematic, complex and discursive in the digital age, so too is the notion of community. As Manuel Castells (1996) points out, communities and networks are reconfigured in relation to geography and the space of flows. Self-selected groups of interest and shared history, rather than simply the group of people that one has found oneself physically co-present among, represent perhaps the most common experience of community in the digital age. Giddens (1990) observes the declining nature of our dependence on time and space, and this is particularly true for the process of media consumption, as well as for the construction of audiences as commodities. Digital and online radio can assemble audiences that are dispersed in time and in space, though this can introduce not only challenges, but also opportunities.

But radio by and for communities of different kinds has been a strong thread, in particular throughout the recent history of radio – and indeed the extent to which these instances of radio have anything really in common with each other depends on the understandings of notions of community more than on the specific manifestations of radio and its technologies of broadcast, institutional forms, economic bases, or types of broadcast text.

> There is no one definition of community radio; however, it is generally understood to encompass stations that embrace participatory, open, not-for-profit practices, and made by and for the community primarily by voluntary labour values. It is a source of local, neighbourhood-based news, entertainment and information. It is radio run for its own sake, for the benefit of the community, rather than for the profit of station owners. (Coyer et al. 2007: 130)

Ranging in kind from hobbyist, low-power FM 'guard band' stations that barely cover a couple of square miles of inner city New Zealand suburbs to the wide-reaching and well-established radio stations serving the rural communities of Australia; from the pirate radio stations introducing new musical sounds to the streets of London to the voluntary stations that give inmates a voice and newfound skills within prisons; from the informational broadcasts that provide important health, agricultural and development messages in small Ethiopian villages; to the voice of political dissent within some small American towns – community radio is a catch-all phrase for those instances, applications and implementations of radio broadcasting that fill the gaps. Where commercial radio cannot find a profit, where major national public broadcasters cannot allocate airtime in their quest for universal accessibility, and where localism (in both its strict geographic and its metaphorical sense) is of greatest importance, community radio strives to meet that human need to hear one's own culture reflected back and to create the opportunity to speak and be heard. Article 19 of the United Nations' Universal Declaration of Human Rights (United Nations 1948) states:

> Everyone has the right to freedom of opinion and expression; this right includes freedom to hold opinions without interference and to seek, receive and impart information and ideas through any media and regardless of frontiers.

That is, not simply to receive but also to impart information and ideas through any medium. Community radio exists, in part, in order to begin to address this fundamental and universal human right. According to Steve Buckley, president of the World Association of Community Radio Broadcasters,

> Community radio is the voice of the people. Community radio is our own radio; it's not somebody else's radio. Community radio is radio that belongs to us. A Community radio station isn't just a space where people can speak; it's where they can really speak out about issues that concern them and their lives. The type of programming that emerges will just sound completely different. I think people will find that it's something that they can really call their own. They will hear their family and friends on the airwaves and really know that that radio station belongs to them. (Kochhar 2008)

But radio has the capacity to go beyond imparting a feeling of belonging and developing a sense of shared identity. The practice of making radio comes as the result of a sharing of practical skills, a process of personal development and the permission and confidence to speak publicly. In their study of prison radio, Grimes and Stephenson (2012: 183) noted that 'the process of skill acquisition is an important part of the process of rehabilitation' and that 'through the supply of information and development of radio production and transferrable skills, individual prisoners are empowered. . .'.

Different schemes for different kinds of community radio exist the world over. Some of them take place within closed communities such as individual prisons or high schools, and others reach communities that are spread over vast areas and are incredibly diverse. The technologies of control (such as the legal framework) that are applied to the community radio sphere differ greatly from place to place – though, once again, they are managed at the level of the nation state. For instance,

> Licensing in Britain allows for stations that serve both geographic communities (like Forest of Dean Community Radio, the only local service broadcasting throughout the Forest) and 'communities of interest' (like Takeover Radio in Leicester, the first children's station in the UK). (Coyer et al. 2007: 115)

But in the sphere of community radio perhaps more than in any other sphere of media, the technologies of control are frequently transgressed, in acts of civil disobedience, and the laws pertaining to broadcasting are frequently ignored or deliberately broken. Pirate radio stations provide a good example of this; but so too do radio 'barnraisings', which take place when volunteers seek to help small, often remote communities that do not have their own community media outlet establish a radio station, often in contravention of the laws of the land.

Starting a radio station is generally considered to be something difficult, expensive and technically challenging – and in most contexts it is. There are, as Wall (2005) points out, high fixed costs associated with legitimately starting a broadcast, over-the-air radio station. But starting a radio station legitimately is not the only way of starting a radio station, as Steve Buckley, president of the World Association of Community Radio Broadcasters, explains to journalist Piya Kochhar:

> What I discovered during my pirate broadcasting days, was that it was not so difficult to actually become a radio broadcaster. I mean we didn't really pay any money to start our radio station we just cobbled together a few easily accessible bits of electronics, built a transmitter, and went on the air. So I realised that broadcasting didn't have to be medium of the elite. It didn't have to be something inaccessible. We could actually take control of this media [sic]; we could appropriate it for community use. (Quoted in Kochhar 2008)

It is beyond the scope of this book to delve in any great depth into the broad range of community radio that currently exists, let alone develop a coherent narrative about its history, meaning or cultural impact. However, there are two questions that require addressing within the context of a book about radio in the digital age. The first enquires about the potential uses and impacts of digital technologies for community radio stations and about the opportunities for further community radio endeavours grounded in the digital media environment. The second, and perhaps more important question relates to the extent to which radio practitioners and scholars in general can learn from community radio and apply their knowledge in other fields of digital media. That is, given the affordances and opportunities of the digital environment, are there things that community radio already does (or aspires to do) that might inspire a different response to the media environment from what those with a commercial or national public broadcast might ordinarily be predisposed to consider?

In response to the first question, activists in the United States have considered digital technologies of networking rather than analogue technologies of distribution to meet the same needs as community radio, without the severe restrictions often imposed by the legislative framework. By recasting community media as connectivity and conversation rather than as broadcasting, they approach the right to impart and receive information and ideas as well as the opportunity to hear their own culture and community reflected back in a horizontally connected fashion, through the linking of personal, open wi-fi networks, in an array within a small, geographically defined area.

> While the activists deem FM radio as appropriate and desirable for community groups, due to a limitation placed by Congress in 2000, LPFMs are virtually impossible to license in US cities; spectrum is perceived to be scarce and it is often impossible to meet the spacing requirements for new LPFMs. Partly due to the unavailability of LPFM as an option, Pandora organizers considered the utility of community wi-fi networks in cities. (Dunbar-Hester 2009: 227)

As an approach, the concept has advantages, and also takes an affordance of the digital environment and its technologies into account in order to address needs similar to those that community radio would address. While there are many examples of online streaming and podcast audio texts that replicate and support community radio ideals, these have the disadvantage of relying heavily on infrastructure that is not publicly owned. As Meinrath (2005: 230) observes, 'the term "community wireless network" indicates "open, freely accessible, nonproprietary systems" . . .', which would allow for greater opportunities for dialogue, media creation and sharing over networks that are not controlled by telecommunications and corporate media companies in the way the basic infrastructure of the consumer internet is currently configured.

In response to the second question, an example from my own listening is instructive. I wrote a blog post about a news bulletin I heard on a small local community hip-hop and urban music station in my home town of Auckland. As the young newsreader presented the bulletin, she was interrupted by the programme's host, who engaged her in dialogue and contributed personal reflection and some expert knowledge about the context and other socio-political factors relating to the news story. The discussion directly related to and affected the audience of that station, and the knowledge and background that was shared on air as a result of that exchange was one in which understanding was prioritised over the relating of facts and events. The conventions of 'traditional' broadcasting, in which the news is treated as separate from the programme content, presented as facts that are canonical and above interrogation, and delivered with a degree of formality, were completely broken in that exchange, in a way that one is usually only likely to find in the context of community radio. However, with respect to the broader political economy of media in search of the greater public and social good, the change in the media environment provides a moment in time and an opportunity to reflect upon the kinds of things that we might wish for our media to accomplish in the digital age – and this might be just one example of the kinds of practices that enhance our ability to ensure that fundamental human right of expression and access to knowledge.

In other words, through that frankly brief but significant exchange, the broadcasters were exercising their democratic right. And whether they did it well or badly, simple, profound and meaningful new things come from the margins in radio – and in culture generally. Broadcasters and policy-makers who believe that community radio is important because the next generation of talent will be trained in that field and will emerge from that milieu overlook the more significant fact that – today more than ever – this is the place from which the disruptive challenge to the formulas, monolithic structures and conventions of radio will emerge. Community radio – and particularly small community radio – is a space where new ways of making media are attempted, experiments are tried, and the economics and regulatory frameworks are more enabling and nurturing to these kinds of practices.

In searching for new responses to the digital environment, community radio – whether online or over the air – provides a space for these ideas to seed and take hold, so that those approaches to the media environment – not simply the raw human resource talent – can be harvested and the benefits reaped for the whole society.

CHAPTER EIGHT

Don't Touch That Dial (What Dial?)

At a panel at WFMU's 2011 Radiovision Festival, radio broadcaster Ira Glass was asked a question about the future of radio, and particularly about the future of the craft of radio. His initial response was generally positive and suggested that, as long as people continued to drive to work and were lazy about their media choices, there would be a reason for there to be something for them just to switch on habitually. Radio, he suggested, would survive simply because things continue in the absence of a reason for them not to. But, considering further, his response changed. The problem was not that the answer was unsatisfactory, but rather that the question was meaningless.

> I feel like, as a people, we have to officially stop asking if radio is going to survive. It's so boring! I feel like I get asked that, like, every two weeks of my life, and the fact is we don't have to decide that. You know what I mean? We don't have to come to a judgment on that. . . . I don't think we have to worry. If radio goes away, something else will happen, and who gives a fuck that it's gone? (Ira Glass, quoted in Phelps 2011)

Radio in the digital age is still just radio to the extent that we think of it as being radio. There may well be aspects of its production and distribution chain that remain analogue. The context in which it is situated, the tools with which it is created, the political economy that shapes its institutions and the ways in which we consume it may differ. But fundamentally – and tautologically – radio is radio. We still talk about devices, transmissions, texts and subtexts, audiences, stations, political economies, production technologies, professional practices and promotional cultures. The details of the discussions that broadly fall under these categories may be entirely different, but it is largely the same set of conversations we are having. Whatever radio might happen to be, it is the age that is digital.

But, while radio is a complex, discursive and contested area of study, it is nonetheless something that most people feel they have a reasonable familiarity with and understanding of. Radio is what I listen to when I get into my car. This is a radio documentary or radio drama, which distinguishes it from a television or film documentary or drama. This person is a radio producer. This streaming service is radio; that one is not. This podcast is radio; that one is not. This device on my kitchen bench on which I can listen to BBC Radio 4 is a radio; this device in my pocket on which I can listen to BBC Radio 4 is not a radio. And so on. Definitions elude us, but certainty does not appear to.

But, ultimately, it doesn't matter whether we call 'radio' one thing or another – or even if radio exists at all in any recognisable form. While it seems to be a truism that no medium ever really dies, but rather gets shifted around among other, newer media, in a re-shuffling of ratios, the 'death of radio' is neither something to be feared nor indeed a concept that really has any particularly useful meaning. Human beings communicate with each other. We tell stories, we share songs, we teach and we learn, we impart and receive information – and we do so using a range of tools, techniques and aesthetic choices that are made available to us within a particular media environment, mostly within the boundaries of legal frameworks and other forms of restriction and technologies of control, for reasons of public good, profit or community cohesion.

The New Mythic Age of Radio

In Northrop Frye's *Anatomy of Criticism* (1957), a central premise is that literature has gone through several distinct modes throughout its history and that these are archetypes that we can observe at play in the kinds of stories we tell throughout history.

Frye identifies them as the mythic, romantic, high mimetic, low mimetic and ironic modes – in this order. The journey throughout literary civilisation, then, has been something of a descent from Homer's tales of the gods down through grandiose heroes of the real world to the inner workings and intrigues of high society, to the everyday challenges of low society, and ultimately to the depersonalising and oppressive worlds of Beckett and Kafka. And each phase has its characteristics, its ways of treating its protagonists, its interpretations of comedy and tragedy, and its ways of understanding and representing the world.

Frye argues that, if you descend through the five phases – and keep going – you push down past the ironic phase and you end up back in the mythic phase again. In fact Frye suggests that this has happened more than once already, in a cyclical history of narrative. Each journey through the cycle has the added advantage of experience, and its thematic content is tied more closely to our own contemporary times – our own media environment. One way to think about this progression through the range of archetypes is to consider the way in which this pattern of storytelling plays out within our own contemporary world of popular, mainstream media. While culturally speaking we may not be as interested in mythologies of gods and monsters as we once were (nor are we so big on epic poetry), as a society we do appear to be quite keen on 3-hour-long movies about superheroes. Arguably these can be viewed as our contemporary popular culture's equivalent of epic mythical tales. But, importantly, the stories are in themselves a reappraisal of mythic narrative through experienced eyes. In other words, we find ourselves retelling the same stories from the beginning again. The movie franchise reboot is our latest incarnation and mainstream equivalent of origin myths. Batman is no longer the comedic romantic lead played by Adam West, whom we encountered in our age of televisual innocence. He is now the cinematic Dark Knight whom we revisit through the post-ironic eyes of experience. This is the story that we can now relate to; that we can return to with wisdom, and worldliness – not with naïveté and wonder.

And, as for radio, the media environment provides affordances for a similar reinvention of storytelling and of our own adaptations in response to the ecology in which that storytelling takes place. But we can also consider this trajectory as emblematic of the medium's path, through history, to where we are today. To attempt – admittedly fairly clumsily – to map the trajectory of radio in the electric age onto Frye's modes of literature is, in a sense, an exercise in the arbitrary attribution of patterns and meanings where none may appear to exist – but this is one of the ways in which we make sense of things. We join the dots, look for connections and come to understandings on the basis of frameworks that may, at best, be only coincidentally similar. And yet this process helps to open up understanding. So, in order to provide a way in which to explain the emergence of radio into the digital age as a process of transcendence, I propose that we have passed through the crystal age of mythical voices in the air and through the so-called 'golden age' of radio heroes. We have moved through the high mimetic, high-society representations of culture and aspirations of cultural uplift on air. We have passed through the low mimetic representations of the everyman through the medium of voxpop, the representations of the taste and humour of the ordinary and the proliferation of the popular song as the heart and soul of radio for the masses. And now we emerge through the ironic, almost dehumanised Kafka-esque nightmare of hyperformatted, personality-less radio. But we find ourselves in freefall in the digital age. We have emerged beneath a hierarchy of modes, looking for ways to interpret and communicate – searching for what is of interest, what might be possible, what is of significance, what affordances and effectivities shape our responses and what stories may be told. The path we walked, in our innocence, we can now return to, having seen and understood where it leads. All of the things that brought us to radio in the first place – we can now go back to them and attempt them again. To tell our own origin stories in a post-ironic age.

Perhaps not to continue to make countdowns of the most popular hits of the year, but still to make programmes as if music matters. Not to make radio comedies that rehash the same territory or use the same techniques as, say, *The Hitchhiker's Guide to the Galaxy*, but rather to tell new stories in new ways, which genuinely understand the technological and cultural milieu. Not to make programmes that terrify pre-teens about the impending nuclear holocaust, but perhaps engage them in an equally (or perhaps more) effective way – and also in an empowering way – in genuine global threats and political issues that they can be informed about, engaged in, connected to and proactive about. Perhaps we could even give them a voice, so that they may engage in their democratic and universal human right.

Radio as a mythic force – that same mythic force that shaped both my imagination as a child and to a large extent the person I have become as an adult – is back. It's already back. Most of us haven't noticed it yet, because it is emerging from the margins. Many radio professionals, radio amateurs, radio listeners and radio academics are, I would suggest, still in freefall – looking backward, reminiscing about an age of radio that was better than it is today in some way, shape or form, perhaps an age when radio was something we had a job in and knew where we stood. It wasn't better then, I would venture – but this is how we interpret the world. What we have the opportunity to do is consider the affordances of the digital age, return to first principles about what it is we wish to achieve with our media and communications and, as a society, work and agitate to develop that as best we can. Whether or not we call 'radio' what we make as a result is immaterial. Radio is a means and not an end.

The purpose of this book is not to celebrate radio's longevity or to eulogise a lost media form. The book does not attempt to answer questions or solve problems to do with radio in the digital age, because that would be an attempt to shut down dialogue in a vibrant, interesting and important area of media studies. Instead this book has sought at least to begin to lay out a range of areas in which conversations about radio and media can be opened and explored. As one commentator noted on Twitter, it's complicated:

> #Radio is dead. Unless you count the fact that it's in every car and home in the world & streaming to mobile devices/desktops. All for free. (Drunk Jock 2012)

Radio has not simply 'been digitalised', but instead digitalisation has taken place at a far broader societal level, and this dominant technological and cultural force entirely recontextualises the medium in a new ecological frame. Our understanding of the processes underpinning that change and of the new context allows for a creative response to the media environment; and in so doing it also offers new ways of understanding, making and consuming radio.

I am optimistic about radio, although it is not radio that I care for but the human act of communication that shares and shapes our understanding and experiences, that marks out our daily routines, that allows us to engage in democratic and artistic processes and that provides us with meaning, human connection and, simply, something to talk about.

> If television and radio are merely appliances, then their fate is sealed. If they are simply methods of distribution via radio waves, then their place in the new media environment is one of marginalisation. If they are a type of programming, then they are but one type among an increasing diversity of interests and their possible gratifications. If, however, they are also professional and quality contexts for communication, education, discussion, entertainment, representation and engagement, then they will no doubt provide a welcome part of the contemporary media ecology. (Brown and Dubber 2007)

I imagine myself as being that same young person who grew up on radio, but growing up instead in today's media environment; and I wonder what would be lost or gained from that transposition. It's hard to say, but I would like to think that many of the same kinds of memories and meanings would emerge. They would be recognisable in some ways, entirely transformed in others. Radio was and remains incredibly important to me and to many others all over the world. Is that as true today as it was in the last decades of the twentieth century? Will it be as true in decades to come? Indeed – does it matter?

While I'm reluctant to get into the realm of fortune telling or into predicting the future of radio (predicting the future of any-thing is a guaranteed method of appearing foolish when it comes to putting words in print), I think McLuhan's reminder that 'the medium is the message' is apropos. Not that the message is unimportant, because, as we've established, the medium's content can have a profound and lasting effect on its recipients and on the shared cultural context. Not that the medium of radio is the whole point of anything, either. I do not invoke McLuhan's provocation in order to champion an essentialist or received version of what radio is, as if it has some kind of magical quality that marks radio out for special treatment or preservation – but rather to stress that it is the media context that we should be paying attention to.

As I have said at the very beginning, this is not a book about digital radio. In fact it's not really even a book about radio. Rather, through radio as a series of discursive practices and categories, we have the opportunity to examine the digital age: the media context within which we are all currently situated. Its shifting ground, the affordances and restrictions that con-text imposes, and the kinds of responses we can have to it as a society, as media producers, as critical audiences and as par-ticipants in a mediated conversation that is no longer exclusively allocutionary.

Radio is important exactly to the extent that we thought we understood what it was, and now it becomes apparent that we never did. It appeared to have essential characteristics that turn out to be instead socially and politically negotiated norms, enabled by an earlier technological environment. When placed in the context of the new technological environment, our under-standing of how radio works – or even where its boundaries lie – call into question our understanding of media more generally: how media work on us, how we respond to them, how they can be used, how they should be regulated, and so on.

In other words, radio is crucially important as a media form now, more than ever before, precisely because it has become apparent that it might not be important at all. And, by letting go of our received and inherited notions of 'how radio works' and rather approaching the digital media environment on its own terms, we have the opportunity to invent radio all over again – or possibly something else. It doesn't really matter what it gets called. But by understanding radio in the digital age we have the opportunity to apply its techniques, its power as a musical form, its storytelling strengths, its emancipatory potential for community participation and democracy, and its meanings and significances for practitioners and audiences alike – in whole new ways.

Whatever becomes of the media form we have collectively called 'radio' for the past hundred or so years, its legacy will no doubt continue to echo in a variety of different ways as we carry its lessons forward. Some of those things will, no doubt, continue to be called radio. And arguments about whether those things are correctly defined as such will no doubt continue to exercise those to whom it matters, will distract scholars and will generate popular discourse. And that, in itself, I think, is interesting – it is *the* interesting bit.

References

Abbott, H. P. (2008) *The Cambridge Introduction to Narrative* (2nd edn). Cambridge: Cambridge University Press.

Adams, D. (1998) What have we got to lose? At http://www.douglasadams.com/dna/980707-05-a.html (accessed 9 October 2012).

Adorno, T. W. (1945) A social critique of radio music. *The Kenyon Review,* 7(2), 208–425.

Ahlkvist, J. A. (2001) Programming philosophies and the rationalization of music radio. *Media, Culture & Society,* 23, 339–58.

Ala-Fossi, M. and Stavitsky, A. G. (2003) Understanding IBOC: Digital technology for analog economics. *Journal of Radio Studies,* 10, 63–79.

Ala-Fossi, M., Lax, S., O'Neill, B., Jauert, P. and Shaw, H. (2008) The future of radio is still digital – but which one? Expert perspectives and future scenarios for radio media in 2015. *Journal of Radio & Audio Media,* 15, 4–25.

Alper, G. (2006) XM reinvents radio's future. *Popular Music and Society,* 29, 505–18.

Alper, G. (2012) Personal email communication.

Anderson, C. (2006) *The Long Tail: Why the Future of Business is Selling Less of More.* New York: Hyperion.

Banerjee, I. and Seneviratne, K. (2006) *Public Service Broadcasting in the Age of Globalization.* Jurong Point, Singapore: Asian Media Information and Communication Centre (AMIC).

Barham, L. and Mitchell, P. (2008) *The First Africans: African Archaeology from the Earliest Toolmakers to Most Recent Foragers* (Cambridge World Archaeology series). Oxford: Oxford University Press.

Barnard, S. (1989) *On the Radio: Music Radio in Britain.* Milton Keynes: Open University Press.

Barnett, E. (2012) BBC launches tool silencing Wimbledon players' grunts. *Telegraph.* At http://www.telegraph.co.uk/technology/news/8606914/BBC-launches-tool-silencing-Wimbledon-players-grunts.html (accessed 20 December 2012).

BBC (2012) The Listening Project. BBC. At http://www.bbc.co.uk/programmes/b01cqx3b/features/about (accessed 18 December 2012).

Berland, J. (1990) Radio space and industrial time: Music formats, local narratives and technological mediation. *Popular Music*, 9, 179–92.

Berry, R. (2006) Will the iPod kill the radio star? Profiling podcasting as radio. *Convergence: The International Journal of Research into New Media Technologies*, 12, 143–62.

Black, D. A. (2001) Internet radio: A case study in medium specificity. *Media, Culture & Society*, 23, 397–408.

Bonet, M., Fernandez-Quijada, D. and Ribes, X. (2011) The changing nature of public service radio: A case study of iCat fm. *Convergence: The International Journal of Research into New Media Technologies*, 17, 177–92.

Bordewijk, J. L. and van Kaam, B. (2002) Towards a new classification of tele-information services [1986]. In D. McQuail (ed.), *McQuail's Reader in Mass Communication Theory*, 113–24. London: Sage.

Brown, R. and Dubber, A. (2007) New Zealand on air: We're all in this together: Public broadcasting in the digital age. At http://www.nzonair.govt.nz/media/6947/public%20broadcasting%20in%20the%20digital%20age%20oct%202007.pdf (accessed 12 January 2013).

Burli (2012) Burli software: Benefits. At http://www.burli.com/burli-benefits/benefits/ (accessed 8 December 2012).

Castells, M. (1996) *The Rise of the Network Society*. Oxford: Blackwell.

Castells, M. (2006) The network society: From knowledge to policy. In M. Castells and G. Cardoso (eds), *The Network Society: From Knowledge to Policy*, 3–22. Washington, DC: Centre for Transatlantic Relations.

Churnside, A. (2012, 24 March) Interview/recorded private conversation: Audio innovation at the BBC. At http://radiointhedigitalage.com/2012/03/audio-innovation-at-the-bbc/ (accessed 24 May 2013).

CMU (2012) American radio royalties up for debate in Congress: Complete music update. At http://www.thecmuwebsite.com/article/american-radio-royalties-up-for-debate-in-congress/ (accessed 11 December 2012).

Coley, S. (2012a) Bowie's Waiata: Radio documentary and fandom. In M. Mollgaard (ed.), *Radio and Society: New Thinking for an Old Medium*, 83–98. Newcastle: Cambridge Scholars Publishing.

Coley, S. (2012b, 20 December) Unpublished interview/recorded private conversation: Reflections on Bowie's Waiata and online fan practice.

Coyer, K., Dowmunt, T. and Fountain, A. (2007) *The Alternative Media Handbook*. New York: Routledge.

Crisell, A. (1986) *Understanding Radio*. London: Methuen.

Crook, T. (1999) *Radio Drama: Theory and Practice*. London: Routledge.

Cutting, J. E. (1982) Two ecological perspectives: Gibson vs. Shaw and Turvey. *American Journal of Psychology*, 95, 199–222.

Daisey, M. (2012) *This American Life: Mr Daisey and the Apple Factory* (Retracted radio story). USA: National Public Radio. At http://www.

thisamericanlife.org/radio-archives/episode/454/mr-daisey-and-the-apple-factory?act=1 (accessed 10 December 2012).

de Chardin, Pierre Teilhard (1955) *The Phenomenon of Man.* New York: Harper Perennial / Modern Thought.

Douglas, S. J. (1999) *Listening In: Radio and the American imagination, from Amos 'n' Andy and Edward Murrow to Wolfman Jack and Howard Stern.* New York: Random House / Times Books.

Drunk Jock (2012) #Radio is dead. Unless you count the fact that it's in every car and home in the world & streaming to mobile devices/desktops. All for free. (@drunkjock). At https://twitter.com/drunkjock/status/276136808138555393 (accessed 13 January 2013).

Dubber, A. (2007) *Tutira mai nga iwi* (line up together, people): Constructing New Zealand identity through commercial radio. *Radio Journal: International Studies in Broadcast and Audio Media,* 5(1), 19–53.

Dubber, A. (2012) Monkey on the roof: Researching creative practice, music consumption, social change and the online environment. *Creative Industries Journal,* 4, 19–32.

Dunaway, D. K. (2000) Digital radio production: Towards an aesthetic. *New Media & Society,* 2(1), 29–50.

Dunbar-Hester, C. (2009) 'Free the spectrum!' Activist encounters with old and new media technology. *New Media & Society,* 11(1/2), 221–40.

Dunbar-Hester, C. (2010) The history and future of hyper-local radio. *The Atlantic.* At http://www.theatlantic.com/technology/archive/2010/10/the-history-and-future-of-hyper-local-radio/64058/ (accessed 4 January 2013).

Eco, U. (1989) *The Open Work,* trans. Anna Cancogni. London: Hutchinson Radius.

Engeström, Y. (2000) Activity theory as a framework for analyzing and redesigning work. *Ergonomics,* 43(7), 960–74.

Engeström, J. (2005) Why some social network services work and others don't – Or: The case for object-centered sociality. Zengestrom. At http://www.zengestrom.com/blog/2005/04/why_some_social.html (accessed 13 April 2012).

Fairchild, C. (2012) *Music, Radio and the Public Sphere: The Aesthetics of Democracy.* London: Palgrave Macmillan.

Farrar, R. (2009) How long should a podcast be? At http://www.richardfarrar.com/how-long-should-a-podcast-be/ (accessed 9 December 2012).

Flichy, P. (1991) *Une histoire de la communication moderne: Espace public et vie privée.* Paris: La Découverte.

Foucault, M. and Kritzman, L. D. (1988) *Politics, Philosophy, Culture: Inteviews and Other Writings, 1977–1984.* New York: Routledge.

Fox, B. (1991, 20 July) Radio sans frontières. *New Scientist*, p. 29.

Frith, S. (1998) *Music for Pleasure: Essays in the Sociology of Pop*. New York: Routledge.

Frye, N. (1957) *Anatomy of Criticism*. Princeton, NJ: Princeton Univeristy Press.

Garfield, B. (2012) Mike Daisey's betrayal of *This American Life*'s truth – and my trust. *Guardian*. At http://www.guardian.co.uk/commentisfree/ cifamerica/2012/mar/17/mike-daisey-this-american-life (accessed 10 December 2012).

Garner, K. (1990) New gold dawn: The traditional English breakfast show 1989. *Popular Music*, 9, 193–202.

Gibson, J. J. (1977) The theory of affordances. In R. Shaw and J. Bransford (eds), *Perceiving, Acting, and Knowing: Toward an Ecological Psychology*, 67–82. Hillsdale, NJ: Lawrence Erlbaum.

Giddens, A. (1990) *The Consequences of Modernity*. Stanford: Stanford University Press.

Given, J. (1998) *The Death of Broadcasting: Media's Digital Future*. Sydney: UNSW Press.

Glass, I. and Chicago Public Media (2011) *The Invisible Made Visible* (episode of *This American Life*). At http://live.thisamericanlife.org/ (accessed 19 December 2012).

Glasser, T. L. (1984) Competition and diversity among radio formats: Legal and structural issues. *Journal of Broadcasting*, 28, 122–42.

Gräslund, B. (1987) *The Birth of Prehistoric Chronology: Dating Methods and Dating Systems in Nineteenth-Century Scandinavian Archeology*. Cambridge: Cambridge University Press.

Grimes, M. and Stephenson, S. (2012) Radio as a tool for rehabilitation and social inclusion. In M. Mollgaard (ed.), *Radio and Society: New Thinking for an Old Medium*, 179–96. Newcastle: Cambridge Scholars Publishing.

Hanretty, C. (2011) *Public Broadcasting and Political Interference*. London: Routledge.

Harding, A. (2012) The story of Picle. Made by Many. At https://vimeo. com/38250876 (accessed 19 December 2012).

Hazlett, Thomas W. (2001, January) The wireless craze, the unlimited bandwidth myth, the spectrum auction faux pas, and the punchline to Ronald Coase's 'big joke': An essay on airwave allocation policy. AEI-Brookings Joint Center Working Paper No. 01–2. At SSRN: http:// ssrn.com/abstract=286932 (or http://dx.doi.org/10.2139/ssrn.286932) (accessed 20 May 2013).

Head, S. W. and Sterling, C. H. (1990) *Broadcasting in America: A Survey of Electronic Media* (6th edn). Boston, MA: Houghton Mifflin.

Heizer, R. F. (1962) The background of Thomsen's three-age system. *Technology and Culture*, 3(3), 259–66.

Hendy, D. (2000) Pop music radio in the public service: BBC Radio 1 and new music in the 1990s. *Media, Culture & Society*, 22, 743–61.

Ibiquity Digital (2012) What is HD Radio Broadcasting? Ibiquity Digital Corporation, Columbia, MD. At http://www.ibiquity.com/hd_radio (accessed 28 December 2012).

Jensen, J. (2011) Digital radio in 2012: Views from the EBU New Radio Group. At http://digitalradioconference.ebu.ch/NRGForecasts12/NRGDigitalRadio2012_complete.pdf (accessed 28 December 2012).

Kelsey, J. (1999) *Reclaiming the Future: New Zealand and the Global*. Toronto: University of Toronto Press.

Knorr-Cetina, K. (2001) Objectual practice. In T. R. Schatzki, K. Knorr-Cetina, and E. V. Savigny (eds), *The Practice Turn in Contemporary Theory*, 184–97. London: Routledge.

Kochhar, P. (2008) When India gets going. The Hoot. At http://www.thehoot.org/web/home/story.php?storyid=2966 (accessed 6 January 2012).

Lacey, K. (2008) Ten years of radio studies: The very idea. *Radio Journal: International Studies in Broadcast and Audio Media*, 6, 21–32.

Lax, S. (2011) Digital radio switchover: The UK experience. *International Journal of Digital Television*, 2, 145–60.

Lax, S., Ala-Fossi, M., Jauert, P. and Shaw, H. (2008) DAB: The future of radio? The development of digital radio in four European countries. *Media, Culture & Society*, 30, 151–66.

Lessig, L. (2006) *Code: Version 2.0* (2nd edn). New York: Basic Books.

Levinson, P. (1999) *Digital McLuhan: A Guide to the Information Millennium*. London: Routledge.

Lindvall, H. (2011) Behind the music: what's happening to 'on air, on sale'? *Guardian*. At http://www.guardian.co.uk/music/musicblog/2011/aug/05/behind-music-on-air-sale-radio (accessed 12 December 2012).

Lubbock, J. (1865) *Pre-Historic Times. As Illustrated by Ancient Remains, and the Manners and Customs of Modern Savages*. London: Williams & Norgate.

MacLeod, H. (2007) More thoughts on social objects: Gapingvoid. At http://www.gapingvoid.com/Moveable_Type/archives/004265.html (accessed 24 October 2012).

Malina, J. and Vašíček, Z. (1990) *Archaeology Yesterday and Today: The Development of Archaeology in the Sciences and Humanities*. Cambridge: Cambridge University Press.

Matheson, H. (1933) *Broadcasting*. London: Thornton Butterworth.

Matthews, C. (2012a) couple hours work left, straight to soundcheck. maybe get a wee dig in too before my gig. jyes. Twitter. At https://twitter.com/chipmatthews/status/276863845459427328 (accessed 9 December 2012).

Matthews, C. (2012b) Family day out up in whangaparaoa. Mean day. Home, tired. More beer. Twitter. At https://twitter.com/chipmatthews/status/277613058392723456 (accessed 9 December 2012).

Matthews, C. (2012c) Gig guide, cause we care, and so I can live vicariously through y'all *pause*, on @BaseFM Breakfast [Online]. Twitter. At https://twitter.com/chipmatthews/status/276064584606044161 (accessed 9 December 2012).

Matthews, C. (2012d) #NP Minnie Ripperton – Young, willing and able, on @BaseFM Breakfast. Twitter. At https://twitter.com/chipmatthews/status/276751711098507264 (accessed 9 December 2012).

McCauley, M. P. (2002) Radio's digital future: Preserving the public interest in the age of new media. In M. Hilmes and J. Loviglio (eds), *Radio Reader: Essays in the Cultural History of Radio*, 505–30. New York: Routledge.

McLuhan, E. and Zingrone, F. (eds) (1995) *Essential McLuhan*. London: Routledge.

McLuhan, M. (1962) *The Gutenberg Galaxy: The Making of Typographic Man*. Toronto: University of Toronto Press.

McLuhan, M. (1964) *Understanding Media; The Extensions of Man*. New York: McGraw-Hill.

McLuhan, M. (1970) *Counterblast*. London: Rapp & Whiting.

McLuhan, M. and McLuhan, E. (1988) *Laws of Media: The New Science*. Toronto: University of Toronto Press.

Meinrath, S. D. (2005) Wirelessing the world: The battle over (community) wireless networks. In R. McChesney, R. Newman and B. Scott (eds), *The Future of Media*, 219–42. New York: Seven Stories.

Menduni, E. (2007) Four steps in innovative radio broadcasting: From QuickTime to podcasting. *Radio Journal: International Studies in Broadcast and Audio Media*, 5, 9–18.

Mosco, V. (1996) *The Political Economy of Communication: Rethinking and Renewal*. London: Sage.

Mosco, V. (2009) *The Political Economy of Communication* (2nd edn). London: Sage.

Miller, P. D. (2008) *Sound Unbound: Sampling Digital Music and Culture*. Cambridge, MA: MIT Press.

Ministry of Economic Development (2001) Radio spectrum policy: 1461.50–1490.00 mHz band and channel plan for digital audio broadcasting services. At http://www.rsm.govt.nz/cms/tools-and-services/

publications/spectrum-band-plans/spectrum-band-plans-005.pdf/ (accessed 2 January 2012).

Mumford, L. (1934) *Technics and Civilisation*. New York: Harcourt, Brace & Company.

Negroponte, N. (1995) *Being Digital*. London: Hodder & Stoughton.

O'Neill, B. (2008) Digital radio policy in Canada: From analog replacement to multimedia convergence. *Journal of Radio & Audio Media*, 15, 26–40.

O'Neill, B. (2009) DAB Eureka-147: A European vision for digital radio. *New Media & Society*, 11(1/2), 261–78.

OfCom (2006) The future of radio: The future of FM and AM services and the alignment of analogue and digital regulation. At http://stakeholders. ofcom.org.uk/binaries/consultations/radio_future/summary/radio_fu ture.pdf (accessed 10 January 2012).

OfCom (2012) The communications market: Digital radio report. At http://stakeholders.ofcom.org.uk/binaries/refsearch/radio-research/dr r-2012/2012_DRR.pdf (accessed 1 January 2012).

Ong, W. J. (1982) *Orality and Literacy: The Technologizing of the Word*. New York: Routledge.

Page, W. (2010) Economic insight: Adding up the music industry. PRS for Music report. At http://prsformusic.com/creators/news/research/ Documents/Economic%20Insight%2020%20web.pdf (accessed 11 December 2012).

Percival, J. M. (2011) Music radio and the record industry: Songs, sounds, and power. *Popular Music and Society*, 34, 455–73.

Phelps, A. (2011) Ira Glass: 'Who cares if radio survives? Something else will happen'. Nieman Journalism Lab, Cambridge, MA. At http://www. niemanlab.org/2011/11/ira-glass-who-cares-if-radio-survives-something- else-will-happen/ (accessed 13 January 2013).

PRX (2003) What is PRX? At http://www.prx.org/about-us/what-is-prx (accessed 23 December 2012).

Raboy, M. (1995) *Public Broadcasting for the 21st Century*. Luton: University of Luton Press.

Radio Authority (2001) Local digital radio multiplex service licences: Notes of guidance for applicants. At http://ofcom.org.uk/static/archive/rau/ publications-archive/word-doc/regulation/codes_guidelines/dabnogo 401.doc (accessed 14 December 2012).

Riismandel, P. (2010) 14,420 radio stations in the US. Radio Survivor. At http://www.radiosurvivor.com/2010/03/11/14420-radio-stations-in- the-us/ (accessed 28 December 2012).

Rosenberg, B. and Mollgaard, M. (2010) Who owns radio in New Zealand? In A. Cocker, W. Hope and M. Mollgaard (eds), *Radio – Challenges and New Directions*, 85–107. Special edition of *He Kohinga Korero: Communication Journal of New Zealand*, 11(1).

Rothenbuhler, E. W. and McCourt, T. (1992) Commercial radio and popular music. In J. Lull (ed.), *Popular Music and Communication* (2nd edn), 101–6. London: Sage.

Rothenbuhler, E. W. and McCourt, T. (2002) Radio redefines itself, 1947–1962. In M. Hilmes and J. Loviglio (eds), *Radio Reader: Essays in the Cultural History of Radio*, 367–87. New York: Routledge.

Rudin, R. (2006) The development of DAB digital radio in the UK: The battle for control of a new technology in an old medium. *Convergence: The International Journal of Research into New Media Technologies*, 12, 163–78.

Sanders, J. T. (1997) An ontology of affordances. *Online*, 9, 97–112.

Scannell, P. (1988) *Radio Times*: The temporal arrangements of broadcasting in the modern world. In Philip Drummond and Richard Peterson (eds), *Television and Its Audiences: International Research Perspectives* (papers from the 2nd International Television Studies Conference, 1986), 15–31. London: BFI.

Scannell, P. (1996) *Radio, Television and Modern Life*. London: Blackwell.

Shanahan, M. W. and Duignan, G. (2005) The impact of deregulation on the evolution of the New Zealand radio environment. In K. Neill and M. W. Shanahan (eds), *The Great New Zealand Radio Experiment*, 17–46. Melbourne: Thomson Dunmore.

Steward, B. (2012) Euro-chip will mobilize digital radio's future. European Broadcasting Union, Geneva. At http://www3.ebu.ch/cms/en/sites/ebu/contents/frontpage-news/news-2012/11/euro-chip-will-mobilize-digital.html (accessed 28 December 2012).

Stiernstedt, F. (2008) Maximizing the power of entertainment: The audience commodity in contemporary radio. *Radio Journal: International Studies in Broadcast and Audio Media*, 6, 113–27.

Stoller, T. (2012) Foresight, fudge or facilitation? The making of United Kingdom digital radio policy 1987–2008. In M. Mollgaard (ed.), *Radio and Society: New Thinking for an Old Medium*, 149–64. Newcastle: Cambridge Scholars Publishing.

Sweeting, A. (2006) Too much rock and roll? Station ownership, programming and listenership in the music radio industry. At http://public.econ.duke.edu/~atsweet/ASweeting_RadioProgrammingJan06.pdf (accessed 24 May 2013.

Talkington, F. (2012) Tonight's #LateJunction–TerryCallier, HumanLeague, Sidsel Endresen, Kevin Ayers, Inch-Time, Lou Harrison, Kate Rusby@ BBCRadio3 11pm. (@fionatalkington). At https://twitter.com/fionatalkington/status/273845970545029121 (accessed 8 December 2012).

Turner, M. (1998) *The Literary Mind*. Oxford: Oxford University Press.

United Nations (1948) The universal declaration of human rights. At http://www.un.org/en/documents/udhr/index.shtml (accessed 12 January 2013].

Walker, J. (2001) *Rebels on the Air: An Alternative History of Radio in America*. New York: New York University Press.

Wall, T. (2003) *Studying Popular Music Culture*. London: Arnold.

Wall, T. (2005) The political economy of internet music radio. *Radio Journal: International Studies in Broadcast and Audio Media*, 2, 27–44.

Wall, T. (2012) Música popular y radio en el siglo XXI. In J. I. Gallego and M. T. G. Leiva (eds), *Sintonizando el futuro: Radio y producción sonora en el siglo XXI*, 329–55. Madrid: Instituto RTVE.

Wall, T. and Dubber, A. (2009) Specialist music, public service and the BBC in the internet age. *Radio Journal: International Studies in Broadcast and Audio Media*, 7, 27–47.

Watts, T. (2010) How commercial is New Zealand commercial radio: A content analysis of four youth orientated radio stations. In A. Cocker, W. Hope and M. Mollgaard (eds), *Radio – Challenges and New Directions*, 37–51. Special edition of *He Kohinga Korero: Communication Journal of New Zealand*, 11(1).

Wikipedia (2004) Digital. In Wikipedia: The Free Encyclopedia. At http://en.wikipedia.org/wiki/Digital (accessed 15 April 2012).

Wikström, P. (2009) *The Music Industry: Music in the Cloud* (Digital Media and Society series). Cambridge: Polity Press.

Winston, B. (1998) *Media Technology and Society: A History*. London: Routledge.

Zanker, R. (1996) Radio in New Zealand in an age of media plenty. *Continuum*, 10(1), 33–49.

Index

music fans 100
    online 92
    specialist 93
music radio:
    replacing 98
    shows/stations 46, 60, 66, 75,
        77–9, 84, 86, 88

NAB 138
narrative forms 102–4, 109,
    110–11
nation state 154
Negroponte, Nicholas 37
New Scientist 94–5
New Zealand 2–3, 6, 70, 162–3,
    166
    community radio 150–1, 169
    deregulation 160–1
    earthquake 123–4
    'Programmes for Schools' 3
    records 6–7
    society 24
    spectrum management 162–3
news 60, 61, 102, 104, 122, 123–4,
    173
niche audiences 88, 90
niche music 92–3
niche programming 76
noise 38
noosphere 26–7, 33, 35
North American Radio Broadcast
    Data System (RBDS) 128,
    129

OfCom 132–3, 134, 162
on-demand listening 48, 52–3
Ong, Walter 39
online audio content 112
online music services 98, 99–100
online videos 71
O'Neill, B. 95, 130
ontology 26, 36, 128, 154
    media affordances 32, 34

Pandora 99–100
performance royalties 82–3

photofilms 106
Picles 107–8
pictures 122–3
pirate radios 77, 90, 151
playlists 5, 87, 88, 90, 98
podcasts 55–6, 57–8, 140, 151, 173
political economy 19, 104, 121,
    152, 153, 155, 156, 157, 162, 167
popular music 84–5, 86
    public tastes 88–9
pre-digital era 25
production technologies 19
productivity efficiencies 61–2
professional practice 19
programming 51, 60, 66–7, 74,
    75, 88, 102, 125, 130
public broadcasting 164, 167
public good 159, 160, 162, 163,
    164, 173
Public Radio Exchange (PRX
    2003) 121–2
pull technologies 41
push technologies 41

radio 8–10, 175–6, 180–1
    analysis 9, 11–13, 19–20, 25,
        56, 99
    content 50–1, 54, 111–12, 139,
        140, 146
    context 152
    definitions 1–2, 9–12, 14–15,
        20, 25–6, 98–9, 168
    and time 58
radio data service (RDS) 105, 129,
    134
Radio Hauraki 4–5, 8
    Homegrown 6
    and local music 6
radio industries 74, 78, 80–1
    and radio stations 80–1, 83
Radio Pacific 68, 69, 126
radio professionals 2, 62, 67–8,
    70
The Radio Journal 9, 15
Radio Pacific 24
radio texts 18, 19, 51,71, 140–1